JN412010

River of Love

River of Love

Story of Esther & Stephan Choe

First Edition 1st Publication First Print on February 13, 2026

Author Stephan Choe
Publisher Gil Su Jang
Distributed in South Korea by Knowledge and Sensibility
Publication Registration 2012-000081

Designed by Hui Young Kim
Edited by Hui Young Kim
Proofread by Eun Sol Jeong
Marketed by Yoon Gil Kim

Address 1212 Daeryung Post Tower 6th, 298 Beokkot-ro, Geumcheon-gu, Seoul, South Korea
Tel 070-4651-3730~4
Fax 070-4325-7006
E-mail ksbookup@naver.com
Homepage www.knsbookup.com

ISBN 979-11-392-3087-1(03810)
Price 17,000 KRW

copy right Stephan Choe (Junior)
Damaged books can be exchanged at the place of purchase
All rights reserved.

Homepage Link

River of Love

Stephan Choe

Story of Esther
& Stephan Choe

지식과감성#

Dedication

"To our children, Stephan and Timothée; our daughters-in-law, Marie Seungmi and Monica; and the families of Renate & Andreas Schmeinck and Grace & Ludger Sickelmann."

Contents

Ninth Story: **Coworkers for the Studentenmission in Dortmund**

Tenth Story: **God's Work in Dortmund through Bible Study**

Eleventh Story: **Our Family in Bochum**

About Our Love Story as a Blessing Stream for the World

"Jesus answered, 'Everyone who drinks this water will be thirsty again, but whoever drinks the water I give them will never thirst. Indeed, the water I give them will become in them a spring of water welling up to eternal life.'"(John 4:13-14)

Originally, I was more interested in my present and future than in my past. I thought the past was over, but the future would come. That's why I didn't want to think about my past but rather about my future and prepare for it.

However, while I was writing this work, I realized deeply that my and our past, present, and future are organically connected. There was a time in the past when I couldn't dream of my future and lived hopelessly because I injured my right leg. Then, through the encouragement and help of my class teacher in the sixth grade, I experienced God's grace, which enabled me to attend middle school. There was also a time when I gambled my whole life preparing for the university entrance exam, even though my family was poor and couldn't finance my university studies.

Esther Choe could only attend middle school because of the poverty and felt unhappy. She came to Germany as a nurse's aide to earn money and to seek happiness with it. But she realized that money did not bring her happiness. Then she met Jesus, became happy, worked as a missionary, and married me.

Looking back, our poverty, hopelessness, and sadness have been used by God as opportunities to bless us, and through us, many others. This God uses everything we have been through in the past and present as an opportunity for a blessed future. That's why in this story I write about how God loved and loves both of us who felt unhappy with our external situations. I also write about how God helped us live happily, enjoy eternal life, and serve as a blessing to Koreans, Germans, and people around the world.

That's why in this book, I would like to tell you about the love story: how God loves us, uses us as a stream of blessings, and through us reveals the secret of a happy life to many people in the world.

Like the water of the brook that flows before my birthplace or before Esther's birthplace, the stream of divine love will first become a river of love for some others; that river will flow into the sea and then spread across entire oceans for the people of the world.

Of course, our story is about me and Esther in our special situations. However, the key messages of our story can be applied to you, so you can have a happy, eternal life. Therefore, I encourage you to discover and apply these key messages to yourself as you read this story.

I also believe that some readers of this book already enjoy God's blessings of love and know your breathtaking stories. When you publish your wonderful stories as a book or YouTube stories, your children and many others can read, see, or hear them. Your stories will be of interest to your children and numerous people and will greatly help to them to enjoy a blessed eternal life while expanding the happy kingdom of God.

If you read our stories, you will discover some secrets about how God works. I shall mention only three of them here.

First, God shows us His love for us directly or indirectly through our siblings, friends, teachers, and children, especially through parents, wives, or husbands.

Everyone really needs love. God shows His love for us first through those who are close to us. If we know and accept God's love through their love, we will be happy and enjoy eternal life.

I grew up in a poor family, and my mother, brother, and sisters were not Christians at the time. But I grew up surrounded by their love. Their love was far more valuable than material wealth. Afterwards, I received a lot of love from my Christian friends and teachers. After the wedding I was loved by Esther, my wife and a little angel, and by our children. Moreover, God has poured His love into my heart in abundance. So I feel like I'm in paradise on earth.

Second, God leads everything, even events that we consider bad, to our good (see Bible, Romans 8:28). My family was poor, so it would have been impossible for me to go to middle school. At the end of the second year of primary school, I injured my leg, stayed at home for four years, and attended fifth and sixth grade two years later than my peers. However, with the help of the sixth grade teacher, I was able to attend middle school. God showed me His great love by conducting different people and various circumstances like an orchestra conductor and doing His good will.

This God also works for you through different people and circumstances to make you happy and bless you.

Third, I realized that we should help those who have not yet found God's love and are not living happily. To do this, we should tell others about the love we have experienced. Because God loves not only us but others, He has called us to be, so to speak, a stream of love and blessings to help many others recognize God's love and blessings.

Standing water cannot help but rot. If I only receive God's love and blessings and do not pass that love and blessing on to others, my insides will rot and stink. Therefore, we should not only enjoy God's love and blessings alone but also share them with others. Only then will the water of God's love and blessing that we have received not rot but flow through us to others. In this way, God has ordained each of us to be a stream of love and blessing for all the peoples of the world.

The work of God's love and blessing through us may now seem insignificant, like a small brook flowing through a valley. But in the future, it will be a great river that flows into oceans and performs a work of immeasurable blessing for all the peoples of the world. This promise and vision apply not only to us, but to all who understand God's great will and live according to His will.

Another thing I want to emphasize to you is that God's works through Esther, me, and you are not trivial incidents occurring far from the mainstream of God's love and blessing. Rather, they are important historical events that take place in the midst of the mainstream of God's blessings.

To better understand this point, I will also tell you how God brought the Gospel to Korea, how this Gospel was brought to me and Esther, and how it continues to flow, because God has already determined from eternity to use Esther, me, and you as a river of blessing. He has led us to faith, to enjoy a happy and eternal life and to spread this Good News to Korea, Germany, and the world.

For these reasons, I will pray that every reader of this book will experience the wonderful, great will of God, enjoy a happy life, and share the path of happiness with others.

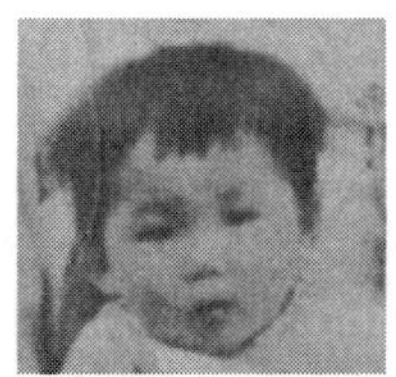

First Story: The Childhood of Esther and Me

"Come to me, all you who are weary and burdened, and I will give you rest."

(Matthew 11:28)

1. Our Birth Dates and Esther's Home

Esther's family photo:

Baby Esther, her parents, her brother, her sister, and her brother-in-law.
Esther with her nephews.

Esther's birthplace is Jangheung, Jeollanam-do(전라남도 장흥), South Korea, about 230 km from my birthplace in Yesan, Chungcheongnam-do(충청남도 예산). Her birth name is Gil-Lye Baek(백길례, 白吉禮). "Baek(백, 白)" means "white." "Gil(길, 吉)" means "happiness," and "Lye(례, 禮)" means "polite." A happy and polite person is perfect. She is truly happy and polite. Her father gave her a beautiful name.

When she was born, her brother was already 14 years old. Of course, all of her family members were happy about her birth. Her actual age is one year older than her official age. Her birthday is according to the lunar calendar. But officially, this date is considered the date according to the solar calendar.

Something amazing: Her official birthday and year of birth, registered one year later than her birth, are identical to my official birthday and year of birth. My birthday was also given according to the lunar calendar. Officially, however, it is considered a day according to the solar calendar.

The same birthday and the same year of birth for both of us show that God had predestined from eternity to bring us both into marriage.

Yesan(my birthplace) and Jangheung(Esther's birthplace)

At home, Esther was called "Song-Ja"(송자) from an early age. Of course, in her elementary school, she was called "Song-Ja Baek"(백송자). But on the first day of middle school, the teacher called, "Gil-Lye Baek!" according to her official family register. She initially believed that the teacher was calling another student and did not answer, waiting for "Song-Ja Baek" to be called. But even though she waited a long time, the teacher did not call "Song-Ja Baek." When she inquired, she learned that "Gil-Lye Baek" was her official name.

Her Korean family name is usually spelled as "Baek" in English or German. A passport department employee probably read "e" as "r" from her passport application and recorded her family name as "Bark." This is why her family name was "Bark" on her old passport. Therefore, her name on the German ID card is “Esther Choe, née Bark.”

After Esther graduated from middle school, she was unable to attend high school due to her family’s poverty. To help her family financially, she attended the tailoring school in Jangheung for a while, run by Mrs. Jung-Hi Park(박정희), the wife of Pastor Nam-Young Chung(정남영).

2. My Mother, Siblings, and My Home

My mother and brother at our wedding in 1977

My Korean name is Myeong-Hwan Choe(최명환, 崔明煥). Choe(최, 崔) means “high,” and Myeong-Hwan(명환, 明煥) means “bright flame.” I was born in a village called Teojinmok(터진목): house number 15, Shinryewon-ri, Yesan-eup, Yesan-gun, Chungnam(충남 예산군 예산읍 신례원리 15번지), a beautiful village about 100 km south-southwest of Seoul and about 30 km from the west coast. To get from Seoul to my birthplace, take a train via Cheonan along the Janghang Line, get off at Shinryewon Station, and walk about 2 km east. My house is where the two mountains almost meet to form a valley. If you continue to walk through this valley, you will reach Sucheol-ri(수철리). The name of my hometown is "Teojinmok"(터진목) or "Teojilmok"(터질목) in the sense that the valley in Teojinmok turns into a field.

Korea was under Japanese colonial rule from 1910 to 1945. Away from Japanese rule, the communist government of Il-Sung Kim(김일성) was established by Soviet troops in the northern part of the Korean Peninsula beyond the 38th parallel. In the southern part of the Korean Peninsula, the US military was stationed, and the liberal-democratic government of Syngman Rhee(이승만) was founded. On June 25, 1950, when I was not yet a year old, North Korean troops stormed South Korea. The Korean War ended with a ceasefire agreement on July 27, 1953. The area where I lived was occupied by communist forces for about three months at the beginning of the war.

The intellectuals and the rich were the targets of communists. When the Allies recaptured our area, communists were shot by vigilante groups, the police, and the army. There is a cemetery about 1.5 km southwest of my house. My mother said that sometimes she heard gunshots from the cemetery when communist activists were shot. Fortunately, none of our family members or relatives were involved in this bloody war because my older brother was still young at the time, and my father was a little too old to become a soldier. That's why none of our family had to become soldiers. Besides, my family was poor and therefore had no reason to be considered bourgeois by the communists. Additionally, my mother's relatives weren't intellectuals either. That's why they didn't suffer much. We thank God for saving our families and relatives from war.

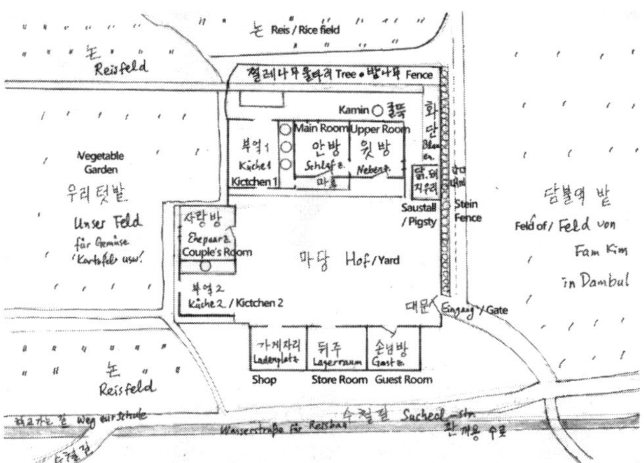

My birth home in 1977

When I was about 10 years old, our birth home had one bedroom, an adjoining room, and a kitchen. After my brother got married, he built a room for his couple and a second kitchen. A little later he built a storage room. In the 1970s, my sister-in-law used the left part of the storage room as a shop. Around 1976, she closed the store and began working as a traveling cosmetics retailer. Then my brother made a room for his children instead of the cowshed next to the storage room.

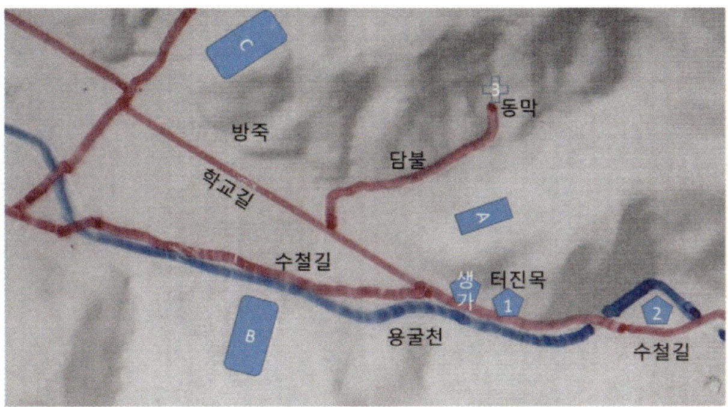

My home village Teojinmok(터진목) and my parents' grave:

생가 : My childhood home

1: **Jong-Man Choi's house**

2: **The Sucheol-ri mill**

✚ : **Burial place** of my parents, grandparents, and brother

학교길(**Road to School**), 수철길(**Road to Sucheo-ri**), 용굴천(**Yonggulcheon-Bach**)

Our Fields: Anan Barley Field, Gaejangsi Rice Field, Chomakgol Rice Field

Neighboring Villages:

동막(**Dongmak**, where Sang-Gyun Park lived)

담불(**Dambul,** where Young-Su Kim lived)

방죽(**Bangjuk**, where Eun-Chun Lee lived)

Villages not shown here: **Garyul**(where my maternal grandparents and their sons lived), **Yonggok-ri**, and **Jaegong**(where Jae-Beom Lee lived).

The path from my birth home to elementary school 7(the bright path on the right)

When my father, Byeong-Lye Choe(최병례, 1910-1951), and my mother, Gyu-Hee Park(박규희, 1914-1979), had six children: my older brother, four sisters, and me.

And I was the youngest. My brother, Yong-Hwan(용환, 1934-2019), dropped out of Yesan Middle School in his first year and began serving as the family representative. The first sister, Gil-Soon(길순, 1937-2000), and the youngest sister, San-Wol(산월, 1946-2019), helped our mother at home; the second sister, Il-Soon(일순, 1940-1995), worked in Seoul; and the third sister, Chun-Ja(춘자, born in 1943), then called "Yong-Soon"(용순) at home, worked in Gwangju. The two came home on holidays such as Chuseok(추석, traditional Korean Thanksgiving Day) and New Year according to the lunar calendar. God first led my third sister to believe in Jesus Christ when she was 14 years old while she was in Kwangju. Through her, God began His work of salvation in my parents' home.

In January 2002, when I visited my fourth sister in Daeryul,

Yesan(예산 대률), she and I drove my fourth brother-in-law's car to visit my parents' grave, which was in Dongmak, Sinryewon-ri(신례원리 동막), near my birth home.

My father was born on December 14, 1910(November 13, 1910, according to the lunar calendar), and died on May 12, 1951(April 7, 1951, according to the lunar calendar), when I was less than two years old, so I have no memory of him. But my mom had often told us how good my dad was. When I wasn't yet two years old, a neighbor had died of typhoid fever. For fear of infection, no one wanted to bury him. But my father had buried him voluntarily. He subsequently contracted the disease and died.

Through my mother's voice, I could see how she valued and loved my father. I never heard her grumble about him. Rather, my mother was full of joy when she told us about him. Therefore, I imagine a happy marriage between my mother and father and am grateful that I inherited the blessings of their happy marriage from my parents. Unfortunately, I didn't see a single photo of my father. He probably didn't take a photo because of the poverty.

If you looked at my mother through other people's eyes, she would just be a poor woman who didn't even go to elementary school and therefore couldn't read Korean. But she was devoted, gentle, and loving to my siblings. I don't remember if she ever said anything negative about me or my siblings. Widowed in the midst of poverty, she never gave up caring for her six children.

She worked in the field all day and asked me to massage her legs in the evening because they were aching from work. My brother and sisters worked with her. After my mother attended a party, she brought home delicious rice cakes wrapped in paper and gave them to us, especially to me.

My mother was suddenly called to the Lord because of a stroke. Before she died, God helped her through my third and fourth sisters, so my mother attended church and believed in Jesus Christ. I heard from my third sister that shortly before she fell asleep on January 19, 1979, she saw the open sky and angels in a dream. She fell asleep peacefully within a few days without pain.

Our God is gracious. I am grateful that God answered the prayers of my third and fourth sisters, saved my mother, and gave her eternal life. Of course, it is unfortunate that my mother died early. But I thank God that he helped my mother, who had worked hard all her life to provide for her children, to sleep without pain within a few days peacefully and enter the Kingdom of Heaven and enjoy blessed eternal life..

I remember my mother, who was like an angel to me. I also saw such deep love in Esther. I can only thank God for His wisdom and love. He blessed us by giving us a wonderful home and conveying to us a heavenly family love through our father and mother. This memory of my mother, Esther's deep love, and our shared faith in Christ formed the foundation of our happy family life.

Back then our house was a farmhouse, and we had rice fields of 1,600 m^2 and some fields for vegetables, barley, and wheat. However, since our rice field was at the foot of the mountain and had to be irrigated with cold water from the mountain, the rice fields only brought in about two-thirds of the normal harvest. Together with barley and wheat, the yield from the rice fields was just enough to feed the family.

Although my father died early, I grew up feeling like I hadn't missed my father because I had a brother who was 15 years older than me and looked after the family. My brother graduated from Shinryewon Elementary School with honors. Mr. Woo-Rin Park(박우린), his class teacher, recommended that my father send my brother to the middle school. So my father sold the family's only calf to pay my brother's middle school admission fee. However, my brother had to drop out of middle school when my father suddenly died of an infectious disease.

Despite this misfortune, I have never heard my brother say anything negative about his life. On the contrary, he worked hard as a farmer and devoted himself to caring for the family. Until I graduated from high school, I dared not contradict his word. He looked strict, but he wasn't truly strict and never hit me. When I was sick, he carried me on his back and took me to Jae-Beom Lee's father in Mulmak for acupuncture or to Dr. Woo-Rin Park in Shilreyewon for treatment. At that time, Mr. Woo-Rin Park had a practice after giving up teaching and studying medicine. I once had an infection in my left gluteal muscle. I remember

Dr. Woo-Rin Park cut the infected area with a knife and placed a medicated wick in it to treat the inflammation.

I didn't dare disobey my brother, but I wasn't afraid of reprimands from my mother or sisters. My mother and sisters loved me because I was the youngest child. When my brother turned 20, he was drafted into military service. At that time, military service lasted about three years. Then my mother wept sadly because she had to take on the difficult work during his military service. Three years later, after completing his military service, he returned home healthy and resumed his work.

Then he fell in love with the eldest daughter of the watermill house. I didn't even see that the two of them were alone together. However, I often saw my brother go to the watermill house and work without pay. Love makes people devoted. Given the Korean marriage customs and my family's economic situation at the time, his behavior was wise. It was very rare in the village to marry after getting to know one another. Marriages were almost always arranged through mediation.

I now think that my brother acted wisely to marry her. At that time, a young man from a poor family would go to the girl's house and help with the mill work to have the opportunity to meet her naturally and gain her parents' consent. When I was about eight years old, my brother and sister-in-law got married in the traditional Korean way. My sister-in-law arrived at our house in a litter that four men carried. You can learn from the Internet that the litter was used for 1,000 years during the

Baekje, Silla, and Goryeo dynasties.

My third and fourth sisters prayed that my brother would believe in Jesus Christ. My brother then attended Shinryewon Holiness Church(신례원 성결교회) and experienced profound joy. God later led my sister-in-law to believe, as well as her children and my sister-in-law's siblings. At that time, I couldn't imagine that my sister-in-law and her siblings would come to believe in Jesus Christ. But God led them to faith in His own way.

My oldest sister worked alongside my mother. She helped her with domestic and field work, as well as with gathering fuel materials from the mountains. She loved me very much because I was her youngest brother. God also showed me His love through her love so I could spend my childhood happily. She then married Jong-Rae Park(박종래), who lived in Sucheol-ri(수철리), about two kilometers from my home.

The Sucheol-ri reservoir is located in Sucheol-ri. On the south side of the Sucheol-ri reservoir is Araemal(아랫말), and on the east side of the reservoir are Yangjimal(양지말) and Eumjimal(음지말). About one kilometer east of the reservoir lies a village called "Saeteo"(새터), the Catholic village. The villages of Araemal, Yangjimal, Eumjimal, and Saeteo belong to Sucheol-ri.

The Villages in Sucheol-ri:

아랫말(Araemal, Below Village); 양지말(Yangjimal, Village on the Sunny Side); 음지말(Eumjimal, Village on the Shady Side); 새터(Saeteo, Catholic Village)
▲ 제 생가(My Birthhome), ⬟ 물레방앗간(Watermill House), ▲ 첫째 누님집(Hause of my first Sister), ⬍ 수철1교(1. Sucheol-Bridge), 저수지(Reservoir)

My first brother-in-law, Jong-Rae Park(박종래), was his parents' second son. He married my first sister and built a house with a kitchen and two rooms in Yangjimal. When I was an elementary school boy, I often visited them and stayed for a few days. My brother-in-law was so generous that he didn't mind my presence. I slept there, and in the mornings, the sun's rays streamed through the hallway, warming me and making me happy. God gave this beautiful nature to this family as a wedding gift. The first daughter of this family is named Young-Sook Park(박영숙). My sister gave birth to other children: Young-Deok(영덕), Young-Bok(영복), Seung-Deok(승덕), and Jeong-Shin(정신).

When I was in Germany, my first sister suffered a cerebral hemorrhage, and God helped her, through my third sister, to believe in Him. Thus, she received eternal life and went to Heavenly Father. Thank God for His grace!

My second sister worked in Seoul to help the family financially. She came home for Korean Thanksgiving Day(the 15th of the 8th month according to the lunar calendar) or New Year's Day according to the lunar calendar. Of course, she sometimes stayed home for a while and helped my mother. Around the time I graduated from elementary school, she married Rak-Kwon Bang(방락권), one of my brother's comrades in the military who lived in Sinam-myeon, Yesan-gun. The newlyweds bought a house in Yesan-eup and moved in there.

My brother-in-law bought ready-made clothes at Dongdaemun Market in Seoul and sold them at the Yesan-eup market, the market in front of Yesan Station, and Sinam Market, which opened every five days. My brother-in-law was a good businessman, and my sister worked with him.

My fourth sister often went to the second sister's home to look after their children and to prepare meals. When I attended to Yesan Middle School and Yesan Agricultural School, I occasionally stopped at the house of the second sister after school.

The second sister has two sons, Yong-Hyeon(용현) and Gi-Beom(기범), and a daughter, Mi-Kyung(미경). Yong-Hyeon attended Inha University in Incheon and the second Gi-Beom Yonsei University in Seoul. The second came to the faith through UBF Yeonhui Center, a student church. Mi-Kyung attended a university in Daejeon and visited the CMI student church in Daejeon.

My second sister suffered a cerebral hemorrhage when I was in Germany. Then my third sister explained the Gospel to her. She believed in Jesus and went to the Lord. Later, the second brother-in-law also began attending church in Yesan and believes in Jesus.

My third sister was called "Yong-Soon"(용순) in her youth, but later, as the family register states, "Chun-Ja"(춘자). After the death of our father, she dropped out of elementary school in the third grade and worked in Gwangju at the age of 14. There she attended Sunday worship in the church and came to believe. That was a significant event because it was the first time the Gospel reached one of our family members. Because my third sister was strong-willed, she held on to her belief, even though she had some difficulty at first. Therefore, God began the work of faith in our house with her. While all family members worked in the fields on Sundays, my third sister went to church first. My mother or my brother reprimanded her, but after attending the Sunday worship, she came back and helped the family with the work.

She married and raised her four children, Young-Ran(윤영란), Young-Gyun(윤영균), Young-Nam(윤영남), and Young-Sook(윤영숙), in faith. With her encouragement, the eldest son, Young-Gyun Yoon, became a pastor and serves the Lord. My third sister helped many people to believe in Jesus Christ. When she takes the train or subway, she boldly preaches the Gospel to passengers.

My fourth sister, San-Wol(산월), is two years older than me. She said that when I was little, I was attached to her, so she couldn't play well with her friends. In fact, there were only three houses in my hometown of Teojinmok, and I had no boyfriends of the same age. My fourth sister is the only one of the four sisters who finished elementary school. She worked in the fields or gathered fuel materials in the mountains for cooking and heating the living room.

She had a big heart. I've never seen her argue with other people. However, despite the efforts of the third sister, she did not believe in Jesus at first. Perhaps because she was kind, she felt no need for the Gospel. But God loved her and gave her the opportunity to open the door of her heart. When she contracted tuberculosis, she accepted the invitation of the third sister, went to the Shinryewon Holiness Church, and believed in Jesus. After that, she served diligently as a Sunday school teacher for children. She also looked after her second sister's young children and helped them with their housekeeping.

When the time came, she married my brother-in-law and served the church with him, the elder of her village church, Daeheung Songnim Church in Daeyul-ri, Yesan(예산 대률리 송림 교회), as the church's "admonisher"[1]. She also raised a daughter, Byung-Eun Lee(이병은), well and worked as a farmer's wife in the fields. After lying sick in bed for a few years, she went to

---

1) **An exhorter(권사, 勸師)** is a person, who serves with evangelism, serving and exhortation in the church.

Heavenly Father in early December 2018.

Just as God made a great nation out of one man, Abraham, God led my third sister to faith and answered her prayer. So God led my mother, my brother, my sisters, and me to faith and raised us as children of God. God will lead our descendants to become a great nation of God, trusting in Him, serving Him, and spreading God's blessings to the world. Amen!

Don't you want to have a picnic with me in Teojinmok(터진목), where I was born? The address of my birth home was No. 15, Shinryewon-ri, Yesan-eup, Yesan-gun, Chungcheongnam-do(충청남도 예산군 예산읍 신례원리 15번지). Now one writes this address as <173 Sucheol-gil, Shinryewon-ri, Yesan-gun, Chungcheongnam-do>(충청남도 예산군 신례원리 수철길 173).

When the water is drained from the Sucheol-ri reservoir, this water flows along the Yonggulcheon brook between Mount Yonggol(용골산) and Mount Deokbong(덕봉산) towards the west.

If you come down from the Sucheol-ri reservoir(수철리 저수지) along this Yonggulcheon brook(용굴천) approximately 1.5 km in a westerly direction, there is the 1st Sucheol Bridge(수철 제1교). The watermill house(방앗간집) where my sister-in-law had lived was just before this Sucheol Bridge. Today there is a folklore museum. This water flowed from a point about 50 m east of the watermill, through a canal towards the watermill, fell onto the waterwheel, turned the waterwheel, and then flowed further into the brook. The waterwheel was about 2.5 m in diameter but would no longer rotate if the water was not drained from the reservoir. Then sometimes my friends and I would go into the waterwheel and spin the wheel with our weight. Of course, this was not allowed.

When the water had flowed about 30 meters west past the mill, a concrete wall and wooden sluice gate blocked the water, forcing it no longer to flow along the brook but into a concrete irrigation canal about 1 meter deep and 1 meter wide. This water continued to flow into an irrigation canal about 1.5 meters deep and 2 meters wide near the house where I was born and irrigated the rice fields in Shinryewon-ri. The dam on this irrigation canal served as a pedestrian walkway from my home to Shinryewon Elementary School or Shinryewon Train Station. I took this route to Shinryewon Elementary School every day and then to Shinryewon Train Station to catch the train to middle school, agricultural school, and high school. So I can draw this path today too.

Jae-Beom Lee and I attended Yesan Middle School by train together for three years. He was a Catholic Christian. He didn't lie, and his mind was pure, so I liked him. When I came back from middle school, got off at Shinryewon Station, and was on my way home, I stopped at Jae-Beom's house now and then.

The brook called Yonggulcheon(용굴천), which has its source at the Sucheol-ri Reservoir, flows in front of my house and continues west along the foot of the mountain in the south. If you continue to walk in the direction west for about 1 kilometer along this stream from the house where I was born, you will reach the village of Garyul(가률). There were around 20 houses there at that time; there was also the house of my maternal grandparents, who lived with my eldest uncle's family. Next to it were the houses of my second, third, and fourth uncles on my mother's side.

About 500 meters north of the house where I was born, there was a single house belonging to Sang-Gyun Park(박상균), who was about three years younger than me and surrounded by mountains. Around his house there were various fruit trees, such as persimmon trees, Chinese date trees(jujube trees), and apricot trees. When my right hip was injured, I had to leave school between the ages of nine and twelve. During this time I spent my days at home. However, along with Sang Gyun Park, I often climbed Yongol Mountain(용골산) in front of my house or caught fish and swam in the stream.

If I walked from our house over the 50-meter-high mountain to the north, I came to Ansan(안산), where our family's relatively large arable field was. I sometimes worked there with my mother and sisters. There were many chestnut trees in the Ansan pine forest next to the field, so I picked chestnuts or mushrooms there in the fall.

And at a place called Dambul(담불), 400 meters northwest of Teojinmok, at the foot of the mountain stood the house of Young-Soo Kim(김영수). In front of Young-Soo's house, there was a relatively large square of rice field that was always covered with water. This rice field was converted into an ice rink for teenagers and children in the cold winter. Of course, my mother told me not to go ice sledding so that I wouldn't get injured. But I made myself a sleigh and drove it. When the rice fields were harvested in the fall, I caught the rice-field snails(우렁) there from late fall to early spring, and my mother cooked them for water snail soup. It was very delicious.

3. Gongju, the Home of My Father and My Relatives

My father originally lived in Ssangdae-ri, Sinpung-myeon, Gongju-gun, Chungcheongnam-do (충청남도 공주군 신풍면 쌍대리). My brother and my first to third sisters were born there. I have never visited relatives in Gongju(공주). However, my mother occasionally visited relatives there, and my grandfather's younger brother in Gongju visited us occasionally and stayed with us for a few days.

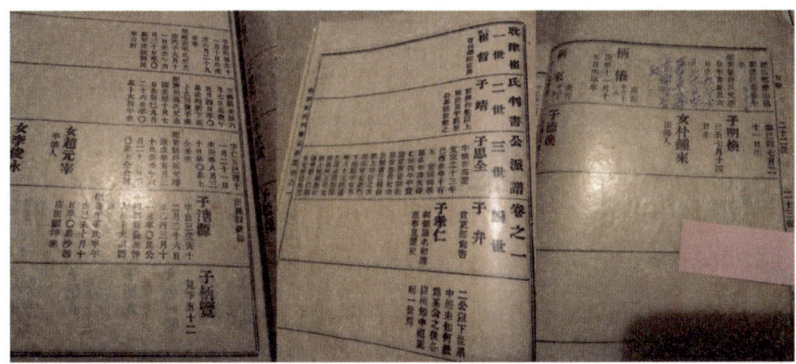

The Genealogy of Tamjin-Choes: The Record of the Tribal Father, and my grandfather, father, and me.

Cheol Choe(최철, 崔哲) was the tribal father of Tamjin Choe, who was the first generation. Dang-Won Choe(최당원, 崔溏源) was my grandfather(20th generation). Byeong-Nam Choe(최병남, 崔柄覽, 21st generation) was my father (but on my parents' tombstone, my father's name is written as Byeong-Rye Choe, 최병례, 崔秉禮).
I, Stephan Myeong-Hwan Choe(최명환, 崔明煥), am the 22nd generation.

Gravestone of my parents (taken after the burial of my brother on Tuesday, July 16, 2019)

On the front side of the tombstone(right picture), it says, "The grave of 'Tamjin' Choe, Byeong-Rye(탐진 최씨 최병례, my father), and 'Milyang' Park, Gyu-Hee(밀양 박씨 박규희, my mother)".
Below stands God's Word from Psalm 23:6, "I will stay in the house of the Lord forever."
On the back of the tombstone(left picture) are the names of the two sons, their wives(Gum-Ok〈하금옥〉 and Gil-Lye Baek〈백길례〉), four daughters and their four husbands, and three grandsons; Gongju, the place of birth of my father; Shinryewon, Yesan, the place of my parents' farewell, and their farewell dates according to the lunar calendar.

According to information on the internet, the Choe(or Choi) clan originally began in the middle of the 1st century with Goheochon(고허촌), one of the six tribal heads of Gaya(가야) in the Korean peninsula. The Gyeongju Choe clan(경주 최씨) began with Chi-Won Choe(최치원, 857 ~?), a descendant of Goheochon. Chi-Won Choe was a great literary master in the late Silla period. From this Gyeongju Choe clan emerged the Haeju Choe clan(해

주 최씨), founded by On Choe(최온, ~ 1170), who had helped the poor well through his aid projects as an administrator in Haeju(해주 목사) in the middle of the Goryeo period(고려 중기). From this Haeju Choe emerged the Tamjin Choe clan(탐진 최씨) with Cheol Choe(최철), the grandfather of Sa-Jeon Choe(최사전, 1067~1139). Sa-Jeon Choe crushed the rebellion of Ja-Gyeom Lee(이자겸) in the late Goryeo period(고려 말기) by killing Ja-Gyeom Lee.

My mother is Gyu-Hee Park(박규희) of the Miryang Park clan(밀양 박씨). My parents moved from Gongju to Shinryewon with four children after my grandparents died when my third sister was about one year old. The reason for the move was that my maternal grandparents' house was in Shinryewon. In Shinryewon there weren't any relatives of Tamjin-Choe, but there were many relatives on the maternal side of the Miryang Park.

My maternal grandfather had two brothers who lived in Dongmak and Bangjuk, but both died early, so I didn't see them. I remember that the aunt in Dongmak had to make a lot of effort to take care of Grandma in Dongmak because she could not move properly.

My uncle Hyeon-Gu Park, the second son of my maternal grandfather's younger brother, lived in an empty room at an orphanage at 92 Gayang-dong, Daejeon(대전시 가양동 92번지) during my university studies. This uncle believed in Jesus through the Catholic Church.

4. The Watermill Family and Jongman's Family

About 300 meters east of my house, there was a watermill house. This house was very closely related to my family because the oldest daughter of the watermill house married my older brother when I was roughly in the first grade of elementary school. When the water from Suchheol-ri Dam(수철리 저수지) was used to irrigate the rice fields, the Sucheol-ri watermill utilized this water, creating power from the falling water on the spinning wheel. The force of the falling water turned the spinning wheel, which then turned the mill to separate rice from rice husks.

Barley underwent a similar process to produce barley rice. The wheat flour was obtained by grinding wheat into flour and then sieving it through a mechanical sieve. The people of Sucheol-ri and Shinryewon-ri 2.-gu("gu" means 'district') used this mill.

Unfortunately, in Teojinmok, where there were only three houses, there were no friends of the same age as me. As a young boy, I mostly played with my neighbor boy named Jong-Man Choi(최종만), who was two years older than me. I also played with Geum-Ja Ha(하금자), the second daughter of the watermill house. She was a year older than me and a clever girl. My sister-in-law had two brothers, Jeong-Nam Ha(하정남) and Bok-Nam Ha(하복남), and two younger sisters, Geum-Ja Ha and Geum-Sook Ha(하금숙).

Bok-Nam is about 6 years younger than me, and Geum-Sook is about 8 years younger than me. Jeong-Nam was about 8 years older than me. He loved literature, so he bought many novels. He graduated from an electronics vocational high school in Seoul with excellent grades. Likewise, he did well on the written exam for an electric company but was not hired due to hemorrhoids and stayed at home. While I had to stay at home with a plaster cast, I borrowed his novels and read many books. That's why, I think, I was able to be an excellent student even after a four-year break from school.

After my mother went to be with Heavenly Father in January 1979, my brother's family moved from Shinryewon to Seoul at the suggestion of Kyung-Sook Choi(최경숙), his second daughter. My sister-in-law led her four daughters, daughter-in-law, and her son(Jae-Young Choe, 최재영) to church and to the faith. In this way, my third sister and Bok-Nam were used as streams of blessing by God. The descendants of my only brother and my sisters will multiply and become a great people of faith.

Jong-Man Choi's(최종만) house was one of three houses in my village. Jong-Man's house was about 50 meters from our house. I played the most with Jong-Man, who was two years older than me. He was the son of an older couple, whose daughter lived in Sucheol-ri after her marriage. Jong-Man was friendly and hardworking. He also had a knack for making handicrafts. Jong-Man's parents were very hardworking. Their marital relationship was also very nice. On winter evenings, when there was not much to do in the country, my mother often visited the old couple; they were about ten years older than my mother.

When Jong-Man's mother died, at the request of his father, Jong-Man married a girl from Sucheol-ri who was about two years older than him; he himself was then about 16 or 17 years old. Their first daughter, Soon-Ju Choi(최순주), was born to this couple. Jong-Man later went for military service and got a driver's license there. After he finished his military service, he gave up farming and started working as a driver in Gyeonggi-do(경기도). When I was visiting Korea around 2010, I heard from my brother that Jong-Man had died. I pray that God will bless his wife, Soon-Ju, and their children. I thank God for giving me a good playmate, Jong-Man, in my childhood.

Second Story: My Mercy Hipbone and My School Days

"So Jacob called the place Peniel, saying, 'It is because I saw God face to face, and yet my life was spared.' The sun rose above him as he passed Peniel, and he was limping because of his hip." (Genesis 32:30-31)

"For God so loved the world that he gave his one and only Son, that whoever believes in him shall not perish but have eternal life." (Gospel of John 3:16)

1. My First and Second Grades of Elementary School

Elementary school in Korea lasted six years, and there was no tuition fee. When I went to school, there were usually around eighty students in a class. After elementary school, children could attend middle school for three years and high school for another three years before going to a four-year university. From middle school onwards, they had to pay school fees at that time.

The main building of Shinryewon Elementary School in the time 1956-1963 when I visited.

Behind the main building were two classroom buildings, one behind the other. The classrooms had wooden floors, so students should take off their shoes. However, the classrooms in the last building had earthen floors, and the students wore their shoes.
Behind the national flagpole, the principal's office was on the left and the teachers' room was on the right.

On March 2 or 3, 1956, when I was six years old, I followed my mother and entered Shinryewon Elementary School, which was about two kilometers west of our home. At that time, first-graders were divided into two classes: one for girls and one for boys. I remember that my class had 84 students. You could say the children were crammed into the class like sardines. What we learned in first grade for a semester was similar to what you learn in kindergarten; we learned to sing and dance. Therefore, young female teachers were assigned to the first-graders as their class teachers. Ok-Ryeol Yoo(유옥열), a young single woman, took over our class. In my class were Hwa-Seop Choi(최화섭), a nephew of the woman in the watermill house; Sang-Man Kim(김상만), who lived in Jaegong(재공); and Eun-Chun Lee(이은춘),

who lived in Saeteo(새터), Sucheol-ri. In the second semester, we began learning Korean and simple arithmetic. The teacher wrote simple Korean letters(한글) on the blackboard, and we recited what she wrote.

At the end of the second semester, we had a written exam. As far as I can remember, it was a Korean exam. I was the only one who answered all questions correctly, so I got full points(100 points). I was a rural kid, and I didn't care if I should do better than other students. And nobody at home had told me that I should study well and get good grades. Hong-Goo Lee(이홍구), one of my classmates, came from a wealthy family. The class teacher appointed him class representative. He was an active student and was well suited to be a class representative. So, I took it for granted that he was our class representative. But because I was the only one who got full points on the exam, this friend made a serious face. So, I thought a little about it. Our class teacher, Ok-Ryeol Yoo(유옥렬), married a teacher from our elementary school after a year

In my second year of school, Mr. Min became our class teacher. I don't remember much about him. However, I remember this teacher hitting a student a little hard for disrupting the class.

When I was in third grade, Mr. Gi-Young Son(손기영) was our class teacher. He liked sports, especially baseball. So we practiced baseball in PE class. For us, third grade students, baseball was, of course, a little early. Because of my hip injury, I only briefly attended third grade.

2. Four Years of School Break due to the Dislocation of the Hip Bone from the Acetabulum

I cannot explain the work of God's grace in my life without describing the incident in which the femoral head of my right leg was dislocated from the socket.

I actually had no problem with my leg until I was eight years old. At the end of December 1957, I was walking home from the watermill house. It was a very cold day. The road crossed the brook about 30 m from the watermill house. At that time there was no bridge there. The place where I crossed the brook was about 1–2 meters lower than the previous road. The water that was supposed to flow from the rice fields on the south side of the road to the brook was frozen on the road. The slope was therefore very slippery. I slipped and hit my right knee on the icy road, causing me severe pain. Since my family was poor at the time, I ignored this incident and didn't seek medical examination. I don't know if this caused the femoral head of my right leg to slip out of the socket.

There was another incident. One winter evening, my second uncle's wife from my maternal side came to visit us. I was lying on the floor sleeping when she and my brother played together. During the play, she pressed her knee hard against my right leg. I woke up crying in pain. My mother and I believed this was the cause of the slipping of my right femoral head(ball) out of the socket.

When I later went to Dr. Schmalz, a bone specialist in Dortmund, Germany, he told me that my femoral head could not be deflected by pressing against my leg. Therefore, the exact cause of the dislocation of my femoral head has remained a mystery.

But God turned my unfortunate injury into a blessing and used it to save me and to bless me and many people.

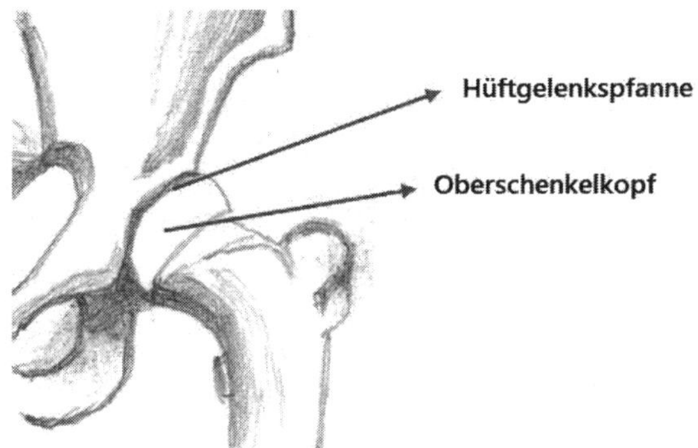

Slipping my right femoral head (ball) out of the socket

The extent of the leg injury was not immediately apparent, but gradually revealed itself over a month or two. And I did not recognize the dislocation of my femoral head from the socket until much later. In Korea, the winter school vacation ended at the end of January. When I returned to school in February 1958, I felt pain in my right knee.

My family was poor then. When my health problems weren't serious, I didn't go to the doctor but relied on folk remedies. Thinking I had a problem with my knee, my older brother carried me to Jae-Beom's father, who pricked an acupuncture needle in my knee. By April of that year, the pains in my leg grew, and I had no choice but to leave school. Thus, I interrupted my school education for almost two years.

After the pause, I went to fourth grade, one class lower than my peers. However, after a week or two, the pain in my right leg worsened to a point where I had to take another two-year break from school. I can't even remember my teacher's name from fourth grade because I attended only for a few days, as the femoral head of my right leg had come out of the acetabulum.

Despite our family's difficult financial situation, I went to Daedong Hospital, the only hospital in Yesan. There they anesthetized me, pulled my right leg, pushed the dislocated femoral head back into the acetabulum, and secured my right hip and leg with a cast. I stayed in the hospital for a day and was carried home afterwards. There were buses from Yesan-eup to Shinryewon, but I couldn't take the bus with my legs outstretched because of the cast. So my mother and my second sister placed me on a blanket and carried me home from the hospital. The distance between my house and the hospital was about five miles. It was around May or June 1960. I still remember the two of them sweating profusely while carrying me on the blanket. They took the footpath next to the train tracks to avoid the dusty car road. My mother and sister must have been very worried about me. I remember their sweating, and thank God for their effort and love.

3. Loved by the Sixth-Grade Teacher

After the repeated two-year school break, I returned to school as a fifth grader in class 5b. My class teacher was called Nyun-Gu Kang(강년구). I asked my third sister, who worked in Gwangju, to buy me a book explaining all the fifth grade textbooks. This learning aid book helped me; it explained the contents of all school books well. When I was in the sixth grade, my sister sent me money again so that I could buy the learning aid book for the sixth grade.

In February, the last month of my fifth grade class, I was checking the cleanliness of the classrooms every day for a week. After checking if their classroom was clean enough, I told them they could go home. I was proud to have this assignment, so I was in a good mood on the way from one classroom to another.

On the way to the check, a teacher asked me, literally, "What are you?" What he meant was, "Why don't you go home but go around school?" I literally answered with a proud heart, "I am human!" The teacher called me into the teachers' room, and he told me to write a reflective letter about my behavior. I wrote that I did wrong. After reading my reflection letter, he said, "You did wrong. So, you should get a few hits for it!" He gently hit me on my shin a few times with a stick and sent me home. This was my first encounter with Mr. So-Hee Yeon(연소희 선생님).

On the first day of sixth grade, a new class teacher came into our classroom. Of many teachers, Mr. So-Hee Yeon was our new class teacher!

Because of my family's poverty, I gave up hope of attending middle school. Elementary school in Korea lasted six years and was free of charge. From middle school, however, students had to pay tuition fees, which were expensive compared to our family's financial situation. Only about 20 out of 80 students in my class wanted to attend middle school.

Mr. So-Hee Yeon made the students who wanted to attend middle school study for another 2 hours after 6 hours of regular classes to prepare them for the middle school entrance exam. Because of my family's poverty, I wouldn't have been able to attend middle school, but So-Hee Yeon loved me. Perhaps he grew fond of me when I confessed my misconduct. He recommended that I prepare for the middle school entrance exam together with other students. He also gave me practice exam papers to prepare for the entrance exam for free.

As the entrance exam approached, he visited our house and asked my brother, who was in charge of the family's finances, to allow me to take the middle school entrance exam. My brother allowed me to take the entrance exam. He also said that I could only attend middle school if I had the highest grade of all applicants and thus received a scholarship.

At the time, every city and region in Korea had a middle school considered the most prestigious. It was Yesan Middle School in Yesan. The middle school entrance exam consisted of written exams and four practical tests: the long jump, pull-ups, baseball throwing, and the 100-meter dash. Simply participating in these practical tests earned 50% of the total score for each test.

When the starting signal for the 100-meter dash rang, I set off with three other students. By the time I had run about 70 meters, the other three had already finished. But I didn't care and ran to the end.

A few days later, the list of students who passed the entrance exams was on the wall of the middle school. Surprisingly, my name was listed first among 480 accepted applicants. I thank God for helping me through Mr. So-Hee Yeon. I am infinitely grateful to the Lord for turning my leg injury into a blessing. He made it possible for me to go from middle school to university and, during my university years, enabled me to have a happy life of faith in Jesus. I am also grateful to God for using me as a blessing to others.

However, I learned that Yesan Middle School had no scholarship system, not even for the student with the best entrance exam scores. My whole family told me to give up my dream of attending middle school. I was sad and wept.

I'll quote an excerpt from my diaries from that time.

<February 27, 1964>

In the morning, I asked my brother if he had gone to Yesan Middle School and asked if my entry fee could be paid later. He replied to me, "If you're not sure that you will pass the scholarship exam, give up attending middle school now. Go next year instead!"

I was upset and wept for a long time. I thought, "How could they not send me to the middle school, even though I had the best results on the entrance exam, and instead ruin me ...!"

<February 28, 1964, sunny>

I was sad from that morning because I was afraid I wouldn't be allowed to go to middle school. My family members advised me to give up my hope of attending middle school. I wept out of sadness.

Then my brother said, "I will send you to middle school. Do you have the conviction that you will always get the best grade among the students? If you only get the second-best grade, you should stop going to school. Swear it to me!"

I answered him quietly with "Yes." I was happy.

In the evening, my third sister told me to give up my wish to go to middle school. But I didn't want to give up in the least.

My brother went to middle school several times and asked to waive the enrollment fee. Eventually, my brother sold some rice and paid a part of the enrollment fee, and I started going to middle school.

In April of that year, I went to Daejeon with my class teacher, Jin-Hae Son(손진해 선생님), to take a scholarship exam for students at Daejeon Girls' Middle School(대전여중). The students who had scored highest on the entrance exam for each middle school came. I took 4th place among the applicants for this exam and received the scholarship, and Yesan Middle School exempted me from school fees. Mr. Jin-Hae Son saved my scholarship so that I would pay my high school tuition three years later.

4. Dreaming of Middle School Years

Yesan Middle School was a public school. There were six class groups per grade, and there were about 80 students in each class group. I was assigned to class group 1C, and my class teacher was called Jin-Hae Son. He remained our class teacher for the following year. Yeon-Sik Kim(김연식), Gi-Jin Kim(김기진), and Yeon-Soo Park(박연수) from Shinryewon Elementary School were in our class, while Dong-Sung Shin(신동성) and Jae-Beom Lee(이재범) belonged to other classes.

At the beginning of the first year of school, my class teacher appointed me class representative. In the second year, the class representative was elected by students. Since the majority of our class group was from Yesan Elementary School, one from Yesan Elementary School was elected class representative. All students took written exams for all subjects twice per semester. Our Korean teacher was Seong-Seon Park(박성선). He was a bit thin, so the students called him "Thinner!" When the students were bored in class, he sometimes told interesting stories.

In the first month of middle school, I walked to school. I had to cross two low mountains and walk about 8 kilometers for about two hours. On the way, I saw the apple orchard. Then I took the train to school. I walked 30 minutes to Shinyewon Station, took the train for about 20 minutes, got off at Yesan Station, and walked about 10 minutes to school. If the train was delayed, the school didn't count our arrival as a delay. As a result, I wasn't late for school once in three years and received an award for it.

Classes usually started at 9:00 AM. After four hours of class, there was a one-hour lunch break and two more hours of class, ending around 4:00 PM. On Saturdays, classes were only four hours long. Of course, in my third year, we had two more hours of class every day to prepare for the high school entrance exam.

Yesan Middle School and I. At that time the playground was not laid with grass.

In order to receive the scholarship, it was important for me to achieve the best grades among students in my grade. Therefore, I prepared math, English, and Korean, which enabled me to understand the lessons well. In my first and second years of study, there were two written exams per semester in all subjects, each lasting two days. I received an average score of 93 out of 100, which was always the highest score among my

480 classmates. The practical sports lessons were somewhat physically demanding for me. I was the only one of the 480 students who had a physical disability. At that time, there were no special provisions for the disabled. Therefore, the teacher gave me grades according to the same standards as regular students.

However, by God's grace, I maintained a positive attitude toward physical education and participated as actively as possible throughout the entire physical education class. If I received a poor grade in physical education, it could be difficult for me to achieve the best grade among the students. The physical education teacher appreciated my active participation and gave me relatively good grades. This positive and proactive attitude helped me avoid being isolated from others and instead build good relationships with them.

In the third year of middle school, class groups were redivided. This time, one special class group of the best 80 students was created from the 480 students and named class group 3F. Our class teacher was Je-Ok Myeong(명제옥). This group also included Yeon-Soo Park and Gi-Jin Kim from Shinryewon Elementary School. Gi-Jin Kim was cheerful and liked to have fun.

The third-graders took exams in all subjects almost every month. The exam results of all students were recorded in order of score on a large sheet of paper and posted on the wall for everyone to read. I always had the highest score on these exams, and Gi-Jin Kim was about fourth. However, towards the end of the year, Gi-Jin Kim took first place once, and I took second.

That made me very nervous. Afterwards, I took first place again. Gi-Jin Kim went to Seoul shortly before the entrance exam and entered Kyungbok High School, one of the best high schools in Korea at the time. After Kyungbok High School, he studied business administration at Korea University in Seoul. Due to my family's financial situation, I couldn't afford to attend a good high school in Seoul.

Yeon-Soo Park was a cheerful friend of mine. He had a pure heart and went to church during elementary school. After graduating from middle school, I attended Yesan Agricultural School, Yesan High School, and then Chungnam National University. After middle school, I didn't see Yeon-Soo Park for about 30 years. Then I met him again in July 2001 in Daejeon when I was visiting Korea. He had become a committed Christian.

5. The Seemingly Lost Two Years of the Agricultural School

My Photos: from Middle School to Graduate School

At that time, almost all Shinryewon students who wanted to attend high school went to Yesan Agricultural Hing School. In early 1967, when I was planning to go to high school after graduating from Yesan Middle School, Yesan Agricultural High School had become an agricultural school. This school combined the three-year agricultural high school and the two-year junior college. I attended this agricultural school because I assumed I couldn't go to university due to financial reasons after high school. So, after graduating from this school, I wanted to take the agricultural officer exam and get a job.

I achieved the best grade among applicants in the entrance exam for this school, received a scholarship, and enrolled in the animal breeding department. As part of the regular classes, we had to spend a lot of time in the fields, such as rice fields. For other students it was natural. But I wasn't happy with that, and I couldn't envision good prospects for my future. My attitude toward school studies had relaxed. I played Go with one of my classmates after school. As a result, my school grades fell, so I was not in first place out of 40 students in my animal husbandry department, but second.

The Yesan Agricultural School later became the Agricultural College of Gongju University and moved to the eastern outskirts of Yesan-eup.

6. Preparation for the University Entrance Exam on Mt. Yonggol and at the High School

At the end of sophomore year, I heard that a classmate from the Agriculture School named Deok-Ho Lee(이덕호), a graduate of Yesan Middle School, had transferred to Yesan High School, a newly established private school. I also heard that Yesan High School would provide a scholarship to a student who passed the entrance exam for a renowned university. So I decided to move from Yesan Agriculture School to Yesan High School and prepare for the university entrance exam.

My brother said he would allow me to go to university if I got a scholarship. The principal of Yesan High School, Seung-Tak Baek(백승탁 교장 선생님), promised me a scholarship if I passed the entrance exam of a renowned university. When I went to Yesan Agricultural School and said that I wanted to change schools, a teacher in charge replied that changing schools within the same school district was not allowed. I went back to Yesan High School and told assistant principal Hyung-Do Choi(김형도 교감선생님) about the reaction of the agricultural school. Then he said if I dropped out of agricultural school, that school would exclude me as a truant, and then I could go to Yesan High School. Of course, I knew that my change of school would have a negative impact on other students at the agricultural school. But I decided to risk it for my future. For me it was like my game of fate. I was never late for middle school and agricultural school. But I intentionally didn't attend agricultural school for two months and studied for the university entrance exam with my friend Eun-Chun Lee on Mount Yonggol(용골산) in front of my birthplace.

Mt. Yonggol was taken on October 21, 1977, in front of my birth house.

The arrow points to the ancient Yongnan-sa Buddhist temple square(용난사 마당), where Eun-Chun Lee and I studied for university entrance exams in March-April 1969.

Eun-Chun Lee was my age and a classmate in the first through third grades of our elementary school. He first grew up in

Saeteo(Catholic Christian Village) in Sucheol-ri and later moved to Bangjuk(방죽), my neighboring village of Teojinmok. I had to graduate from middle school two years later than he because of injury. After graduating from Yesan Agricultural High School, the predecessor of Yesan Agricultural School, he took a break at home. In 1969, he decided to attend the Air Force Aeronautical Engineering College(공군 정비사대학) and prepared for its entrance exam.

Mt. Yonggol is located south of my birth house and is about 400 meters high. There was a temple square of the Yongnan-sa near the summit. It is said that this temple was destroyed by the Japanese police during the Japanese occupation. At that time, there was a rock cave. In front of the rock cave there was a flat area the size of a yard and a small spring. From March to April 1969, Eun-Chun Lee and I studied there day and night for the university entrance exam for about two months, so this place will be remembered forever.

We brought rice and side dishes from our homes and cooked rice in a pot using dry wood collected from there. At night, we lit oil lamps to study. One night it was raining heavily, and we had to move into the rock cave. In this way, God also made precious use of the ancient temple square to save me and many others through the Gospel. Initially, Yong-Seong Seo(서용성) and Yong-Il Seo(서용일) also learned there. Yong-Seong and Yong-Il were cousins and lived in Garyul(가률), about 900 meters from my home. While I was on the mountain for two months, I was forcibly deregistered from Yesan Agricultural School. With a two-year certificate of attendance from Yesan Agricultural School, I enrolled in Yesan High School. My goal was to go to Seoul National University.

Yesan High School and My Photo

When I decided to move from Agricultural School to Yesan High School in the spring of 1969 and prepare for university entrance exams, I never thought of going to Chungnam National University(충남대학교). Attending a private university in Seoul required paying high tuition. So, I prepared for the Seoul National University exam. Seoul National University's exam subjects consisted of four subjects: Korean, English, math, and one elective. I chose chemistry as my elective. But I didn't know whether I would pass the Seoul National University entrance exam or not.

While some teachers at Yesan High School did not teach any SNU exam subjects, I learned one of the SNU exam subjects during their class without listening to the teacher. Once, during history class, I opened a preparation book for the English exam on my school desk and studied English. The teacher called me into the teacher's room and reprimanded me. I knew his complaint was justified. But I thought that I could not follow his advice because of my personal situation.

After this incident, I continued studying some exam subjects in history class but did not show the teacher the reference book. But I knew the teacher closed his eyes even though he knew everything I was doing. I thank him for his generosity.

I studied hard for the university entrance exam. But sometimes it occurred to me that I would eventually die and that all my efforts to pass the entrance exam would be useless. And I lost the will to study for the entrance exam. However, I put those thoughts aside and focused again on preparing for the entrance exam.

Preparing for my university entrance exam was like a risky game for my life. Sometimes I doubted whether my adventurous attempt would be successful. Then I went to Eun-Chun Lee in Bangjuk to discuss our situation. After talking with him, I was able to calm down and focus on studying for the entrance exam again. I thank God for encouraging me through my friend Eun-Chun Lee. I would also like to thank Seung-Tak Baek, the principal of Yesan High School, for exempting me from school fees and paying the Chungnam University enrollment fee through the high school's cash register.

However, around October of that year, Seoul National University announced that all high school subjects, including the second foreign language, were the entrance exam subjects. This was shocking news for me, as I had only prepared for four subjects so far. I immediately bought thin workbooks with which I wanted to master biology, physics, social studies, history, etc., in a short time. I chose German as my second foreign language, but I couldn't understand the German grammar. For example, "der, des, dem, den ..." was confusing to me. In the end, I gave up my intention to take the entrance exam for Seoul National University and took the entrance exam for Chungnam National University in Daejeon, which consisted of only four subjects.

Before the entrance exam for Chungnam University, there was an English exam to select scholarship holders at Daejeon College around December 1969, which I took. Eun-Chun Lee also took this exam. But I failed. This indicated that I was not an excellent student.

7. The Chungnam University Entrance Exam and My First Attendance at the Sunday Worship

In early February 1970, I took the entrance exam for Chungnam National University. The exam subjects were Korean, English, mathematics, and physics as my elective. One of the mathematical questions was one that I had already solved through the entrance exam preparation book. I later heard that I received the highest score in mathematics among the applicants and also full points on the physics exam. The fact that I received the most points among the applicants - that was purely God's grace.

My fourth sister had consistently encouraged me to attend church in 1969. I once replied that I would go to church after the entrance exam. After passing the entrance exam with the best points, I had no excuse to break my promise. On February 22, the last Sunday of February 1970, my fourth sister and I attended Sunday worship at Shinryewon Holiness Church. The pastor preached aloud, so it was foreign to me. I thought that by visiting the church once, I would have kept my promise.

After the worship, the pastor gave me a letter of recommendation to a pastor in Daejeon. I was supposed to deliver it to his pastor friend who worked at the Holiness Church in Munchang-dong, Daejeon. The following Sunday, March 1, I attended the Sunday worship at Munchang-dong Holiness Church and gave the letter to the pastor. After that I never went to that church again. But God answered the prayers of my third and fourth sisters. He also answered the pastor's prayer in Shinryewon and sent me to a student church in Daejeon to study the Bible so that I could receive faith in the Gospel as a gift from God. God sometimes leads us to path we can hardly imagine and blesses us abundantly. Hallelujah!

Third Story: How the Gospel Reached Korea and then My Home Village

"Come to me, all you who are weary and burdened, and I will give you rest." (Matthew 11:28)

"The Spirit of the Lord is on me, because he has anointed me to proclaim good news to the poor. He has sent me to proclaim freedom for the prisoners and recovery of sight for the blind, to set the oppressed free, to proclaim the year of the Lord's favor." (Luke 4:18-19)

1. Arrival of Nestorianism in Korea

Christianity first arrived in Korea in the first half of the 8th century in the form of Nestorianism(경교). This was about 100 years later, after Nestorianism first reached China in 635 AD. Silla(신라) united the three kingdoms of the Korean Peninsula in 676. For this reason, it is estimated that Nestorianism reached Silla around 740 AD.

Nestorians emphasized the independence of Christ's divine nature from His human nature.

2. Spreading Catholic Christianity in Korea and Around My Home Village

Catholic Christianity first reached Korea in the late 16th century. Gregory De Sesphedes, a Jesuit priest in Japan, visited Korea as an escort for the Japanese army during the Japanese aggression against Korea from 1593 to 1598.

However, Catholic Christianity was properly introduced at the end of the reign of King Yeongjo(영조) of the Joseon Dynasty by Koreans such as Byeok Lee(이벽), Il-Shin Kwon(권일신), Ga-Hwan Lee(이가환), and Yak-Yong Jeong(정약용), who diligently researched the Catholic books from China.

Gwangam Byeok Lee(이벽, 李檗) was considered the founder of the Korean Catholic Church, who was born in Gwangju, Gyeonggi-do(경기도 광주) in 1754. He read Western science books imported from the Qing Dynasty(청나라). These books were brought to Korea by the father of the grandfather of the grandfather named Gyeong-Sang Lee(이경상), when he returned to Korea after an 8-year stay in China to accompany Joseon's Crown Prince So-Hyeon(소현세자). These scientific books, written in Chinese script, contained extensive content on Western science, astronomy, geography, and religion. The books sparked Byeok Lee's interest in Western spiritual culture.

In 1777, Byeok Lee participated in lectures and discussions with the young scholars, referring to books by Western missionaries. From this point on, as is well known, he already led an elementary life of faith. In 1779, the Southern Party scholars from the Kiho region(기호지방, i.e, Gyeonggi-do and Chungcheong-do, 경기도와 충청도), such as Cheol-Sin Kwon(권철신) and Yak-Jeon Jeong(정약전), held lecture meetings at Cheonjinam(천진암) and the Buddhist temple "Ju-eo-sa"(주어사) in Yeoju, Gyeonggi-do. There, Byeok Lee gave his lecture on the Catholic faith.

In the winter of 1783, Byeok Lee(이벽) heard that his friend Seung-Hoon Lee(이승훈) was going to China with his father. Byeok Lee visited Seung-Hoon Lee, introduced him to Western science("Seohak, 서학" in Korean), and asked him to meet Western missionaries in Beijing to learn the doctrine of Catholic Christianity and to be baptized there.

Seung-Hoon Lee was baptized in the spring of 1784 by Father Grammont, a Frenchman, as the first Korean. After that, he brought many books, such as the Catholic catechism, the basis of geography, and some objects, such as crucifixes and sacred paintings.

Byeok Lee rented a secluded house and studied and meditated on Catholic doctrine. Byeok Lee was finally baptized around September 1784, according to the lunar calendar, by Seung-Hoon Lee in his home in Supyogyo(수표교) in Seoul. This began the gathering of Catholic Christians, and he began to actively spread the Gospel.

The spread of Catholic Christianity in Chungcheong-do(충청도) was carried out by Jon-Chang Lee(이존창, 1759 ~ 1801) from Yeosaul(여사울, currently Sinzong-ri, Sinam-myeon, Yesan-gun, Chungcheongnam-do; 현재 충청남도 예산군 신암면 신종리). Jon-Chang Lee was born in Yeosaul(여사울) into a technical-bourgeois family that was considered to be the middle class of Korea. At the age of 25(1776), he visited Seoul and was baptized after studying the Catholic Catechism and the Guidelines for Daily Life from the people of the "Southern Party"(남인), such as Cheol-Shin Kwon(권철신), and in the house of Beom-Woo Kim(김범우), Il-Shin Kwon(권일신, the younger brother of Cheol-Shin Kwon), and Beom-Woo Kim(김범우).

He then returned to his hometown, following instructions from his teacher, and diligently preached the Gospel in Chungcheong-do. Although Jon-Chang Lee belonged to the technical middle class(중인), his good relationships with people of all classes allowed him to successfully evangelize many people from various classes. Thanks to his activities, a church was established in Yeosaul(여사울). His efforts spread the Catholic faith most widely in the Chungcheong-do area, with a focus on Yeosaul.

Jon-Chang Lee was arrested in 1791(the 15th year of King Jeongjo, 정조). He was then released for denying the faith. However, he repented of his denial, moved to Buyeo(부여), and once again became active in preaching the Gospel. He was arrested again in 1795 and spent six years in prison. When the Shinyou Persecution(신유사화) broke out in 1801, he was taken to Seoul. He maintained his faith despite all kinds of torture, was sentenced to death along with imprisoned Yak-Jong Jeong(정약

종), and was executed on April 9, 1801, on the Stork Rock(황새바위) in front of today's Gongju Middle School(공주 중학교). He was 50 years old.

Dae-Geon Kim(김대건), who was ordained in 1845 as the first Korean Catholic priest, was the grandson of Jon-Chang Lee's niece. And Yang-Eop Choi(최양업), the second priest after Dae-Geon Kim, was a grandson of Jon-Chang Lee's sister's son. In this way, Jon-Chang Lee's hometown became a seed school for the Korean Catholic Church. Therefore, Jon-Chang Lee is called "Apostle of Naepo"(내포의 사도).

Naepo is regarded as the gateway to the spread of Catholicism in Korea. Naepo here refers to Chungcheong province, including Yeosaul, Sinri, and Solmoe. At the time of the Sinyu Persecution(신유사화, 1801), there were about 1,700 Catholic believers in Naepo. Most of them died as martyrs or fled to other parts of Korea. But many of the believers from the lower classes remained in Maepo, and the Gospel spread among them.

⋆ Korean Catacombs

Sinri(신리), Yeosaul(여사울), and Solmoe(솔뫼) are important pilgrimage sites for Catholic Christians in Korea. Yeosaul is the birthplace of Apostle Jon-Chang Lee(한국의 사도 이존창), who led the spread of the Catholic faith in the early days of Korean Catholicism. Solmoe is the birthplace of the first Korean priest, Dae-Geon Kim. Sinri was the "Catacomb of Joseon(Korea)," where believers lived in secret and worshiped in secret during the period of persecution. Here "Daveluy's Notes on the Korean

Martyrs" were written, which became the basis of the history of the Korean Catholic Church and its martyrs. Solmoe was a haven for martyrs who clung to the Catholic faith and fearlessly sacrificed their lives.

Among the holy sites, the "House of Bishop Daveluy" in Sinri was the place where Bishop Daveluy stayed until his martyrdom in Galmaemot(갈매못) in 1866, after he had arrived on October 12, 1845, on the soil of Korea(Ganggyeong, Jeolla-do) for the first time, along with Dae-Geon Kim.

In Sinri he wrote "A Memorandum on the History of the Korean Catholic Church," "Notes on the History of the Korean Martyrs," and a Korean-French dictionary. At night, he administered the sacraments to the faithful and conversed with them.

"A lot of people have walked to where I am. Breastfeeding mothers, the elderly, and virgins did not hesitate to walk the long three, six, or eight days to receive the blessings of the sacrament. Despite the cold and the snow covering the mountains, they came here. When they arrived, they were exhausted, and their feet were bleeding..."(From Daveluy's "Notes on the History of the Korean Martyrs").

After the end of the persecution, a Catholic community of about 10,000 believers was re-established again in Naepo and Chungcheong-do in the early 1880s.

My birthplace and historical Catholic sites:
내 생가(My Birthhome),
신자촌 새터(Saeteo, Catholic Village),
여사울(Yeosaul, Jon Chang Lee's Village),
솔뫼(Solmoe, Birthplace of Father Dae-Geon Kim),
신리(Sinri, Village of Catholic Martyrs)

Sinryewon-ri(신례원리) in Yesan, where I grew up, is very close to the Catholic holy sites associated with the spread of Christianity in Korea: Solmoe, Yeosaul, and Sinri. From Teojinmok, the village where I was born, to Yeosaul, it is only about 6 km as the crow flies.

And in Deoksan-myeon, Yesan-gun, Chungcheongnam-do(충청남도예산군 덕산면) is the tomb of Prince Gu Lee(이구 대군). He was the father of Daewongun(대원군), and Daewongun was the father of King Gojong(고종), the 26th king of the Joseon(or

Chosun, 조선) Dynasty. When Daewongun was regent for King Gojong, the German Ernst Jakob Oppert, together with the French priest Feron and the American Jenkins, tried to excavate the grave of Prince Namyeongun Gu Lee(남연군 이구) in order to use the prince's body as leverage for negotiations. However, the robbery failed because of the solid layer of lime on the grave.

Because Sinri Catholics were involved in this robbery, devastating persecution ensued against them, and many Catholic believers, such as Ja-Seon Thomas Son(손야선), were martyred. The family members of Ja-Seon Son and his relatives, who had lived there for generations, dispersed to flee. Because of this persecution, the descendants of Se-Dang Son(손세당), e. g., Jeong-Ho Son(손정호) and Youngtaek Son(손영택) fled to Saeteo in Sucheol-ri. There they formed a village of believers and built a Gongso. Gongso was a small Catholic church where the priest was not permanently present but visited Gongso(공소) occasionally to celebrate Mass and administer the sacraments to Christians. After the Japanese colonial period, Sucheol-ri Gongso became a kind of headquarters for the nearby Gongsos in Ganyang-gol(간양골), Gwolgok-ri(궐곡리)(or Gosaeul/고새울), and Songseok-ri(송석리)(or Sugol/수골).

When I was living in Teojinmok, Shinryewon, Eun-Chun Lee's family moved from Saeteo to Bangjuk, Teojinmok's neighboring village. His father was Byung-Ha Lee(이병하).

Jae-Hyun Lee(이재현), Byung-Ha Lee's father, was born into a Catholic Christian family in the 1910s. Because the parents of Geun-Myeong Lee(이근명) and Jae-Hyun Lee died in the

1910s, when Jae-Hyun was 12 and Geun-Myeong Lee was 14. Therefore, Jae-Hyun Lee had to work as a house servant in a house in Sae-Teo, Sucheol-ri(수철리 새터), and Geun-Myeong Lee, his older brother, in Ganyang-ri(간양리).

With the wages from work, Jae-Hyun Lee bought a small field in Saeteo and married a Catholic Christian woman, Yun(윤 Secilia), and had 9 children(5 daughters and 4 sons). Byung-Ha Lee is the 6th child of Jae-Hyun Lee(the 3rd of the sons).

Although Byung-Ha Lee was poor and had to work as a house servant for another family for a time, he followed in the footsteps of his pious, hardworking father. His brother In-Ha Lee(이인하, the second son of his father, Jae-Hyun Lee) became a priest, and his sister Hee-Ha Lee(이희하, the father's seventh child and fourth daughter) became a nun who is currently in the Nursing Home for Nuns in Gyeonggi-do.

This Christian stream of faith in Saeteo, Sucheol-ri, played a role in leading me to Christian faith. Because God moved Eun-Chun Lee, a classmate from my elementary school years who lived in Saeteo, to Bangjuk, about 400 meters from my birthplace. Father In-Ha Lee was Eun-Chun Lee's uncle. When I attended Chungnam University, he was the director of Mary's Hospital(성모병원) in Daejeon. To study in Daejeon, I needed a living room in Daejeon from March 1970. In the winter of 1969/1970, Eun-Chun's entire family moved to Daejeon, and his father worked as the administrator of a former Catholic orphanage(가톨릭 고아원) in Gayang-dong, Daejeon(대전시 가양동). Eun-Chun's parents provided me and my friend Yong-Seong

Seo(서용성) with an empty room at the orphanage for free. Their kindness and help touched me deeply.

During my middle school years, I discussed the possibility of God's existence with my friends Jae-Beom Lee(이재범) and Yeon-Soo Park(박연수). Jae-Beom Lee was an honest Catholic Christian. Yeon-Soo Park(박연수) was an evangelical Christian who attended the Shinryewon Church(신례원 성결교회). He made a good impression on me because he was cheerful and did not lie.

In this way, God prepared me through my friends to believe in Jesus. Their beliefs are related to the spread of Christianity in Korea.

3. Beginning of Protestant Mission in Korea

Now I will tell you how Protestantism came to Korea and spread throughout the country where I was born.

In 1832 the German pastor Carl Friedrich August Gützlaff came to the island of Gogeum-do, Chungcheong-do(충청도 고금도), and preached the Gospel for 40 days. This is considered to be the first Protestant mission in Korea.

In 1865, the English pastor Robert Jermain Thomas, stationed in Beijing, landed on the west coast of Korea and stayed there for two and a half months. After returning to Beijing, he went back to the upper reaches of the Taedong River in Pyongyang in July of the following year on the US merchant ship "General Sherman." However, there he was attacked by the military and civilians of Pyongyang and became the first martyr as a Protestant missionary in Korea. In Korea Protestantism, like Catholicism, was viewed as a Western doctrine, therefore, as heresy, and was not allowed to be spread in Korea.

Missionaries John Ross, John McIntyre, and Alexander Williamson were in Manchuria, a region in northeastern China, and evangelized young Koreans there. John Ross and John McIntyre began translating the Bible into Korean with the help of Koreans.

4. The Mission Door Is Wide Open: The Gapsin Coup and von Möllendorff, the German

In order for Christianity to be properly spread in a country, it must be allowed by the country's rulers and welcomed by the people. Catholicism was persecuted in Korea because these two conditions had not yet been met. However, after these two conditions for Protestantism in Korea were fulfilled, Protestantism was able to spread across the country without significant hindrances.

When Daewongun, who had pursued the policy of isolating the country, had to withdraw from the reign in 1873 and King Gojong(고종) himself began to rule, the Min clan(민비파) of relatives of the queen exerted strong influence over the king. They pursued the policy of opening up the country in contrast to Daewongun's policy of isolation. As a result, the Royal

Government signed trade agreements with the United States, Japan, England, and other countries.

Korea's first trade agreement with Western countries:

Korea - U.S. Peace and Trade Treaty	1882(19th Year of King Gojong): Treaty between Korea and the USA through the mediation of Hongzhang Li, the strongman of the Qing Dynasty

The ruling members of the Min clan, however, were still obsessed with conservative ideology. And Confucian scholars (유림, 儒林), then considered the ruling teachers of the people, opposed Western teachings. As a counter-reaction, young reformists like Ok-Gyun Kim(김옥균, 金玉均), Young-Hyo Park (박영효, 朴泳孝), and Gwang-Beom Seo(서광범, 徐光範) staged a coup on December 4, 1884, overthrew the Min clan, and took power(Gapsin coup, 갑신정변). They sought to break the feudal system and create a modern nation. However, their attempts at reform ended after three days, and the Min clan regained power.

Paul Georg von Möllendorff in official costume as Korean Deputy Minister

Before the Gapsin Coup, Paul Georg von Möllendorff, a German, had come to Seoul in 1882 on the recommendation of the Chinese Hongzhang Li(이홍장). Because Yeong-Ik Min (민영익), the commander of the royal escort and the second most powerful man in Korea, was fatally injured in the head by the assassin's knife during this coup, his life was in danger. Möllendorff quickly carried Yeong-Ik Min to his office and fetched Horace Newton Allen(안련 安連, 1858-1932) there, an American doctor and missionary, for treatment. In early February 1885, Min was almost completely healed. By saving Yeong-Ik Min from impending death as a victim of the coup, Möllendorff gained more trust from the royal family.

Allen was sent to China in 1883 as a missionary from the Northern Presbyterian Church in the USA. When he heard that doctors were needed in Joseon, where there was still no freedom of mission, he volunteered and arrived with his family in Incheon, Korea, on September 20, 1884. There he worked as a doctor at the US consulate in Seoul. He was the first Protestant missionary to settle in Korea.

Möllendorff proposed to the Korean government to build a hospital called Gwanghyewon(광혜원) and to appoint Allen as head of the hospital. Gwanghyewon opened on April 9, 1885. King Gojong(고종) named the hospital Jejungwon(제중원) and sent around 20 officers and servants. This hospital, with the help of Scranton(Methodist) and Heron(Presbyterian), treated about 10,000 malignant patients with diseases such as syphilis and leprosy in one year. This hospital played a crucial role in helping the Korean people trust Western missionaries and open their hearts to the Gospel.

On August 5, 1885, five female dancers(Korean 'Gisaeng') became the first medical students, marking the beginning of the Jejungwon Medical School, which belonged to the Jejungwon Hospital and opened on March 29, 1886. This school was the predecessor of today's Severance Hospital(세브란스 병원) of Yonsei University.

Möllendorff actively invited missionaries. H. G. Underwood and H. G. Appenzeller arrived in Jemulpo(now Incheon) on 5 April 1885. Through Yeong-Ik Min's healing and the treatment of people, God made Christianity a religion accepted by the Joseon government and people. Because of this, Protestant missionaries were able to enter Korea without much persecution, and the door to the Gospel began to open wide in Korea.

Möllendorff also distributed the Bible. During his stay in Joseon, he served as an advisor to the king and contributed to Joseon's modernization by helping to introduce various modern systems such as the education system, hospital system, monetary system, postal system, and legal system so that Joseon could become an independent state.

Then Hongzhang Li of the Qing Dynasty of China recalled Möllendorff to China in late 1885 because Möllendorff did not pursue China's interests but pursued Korea's interests and tried to make Joseon(i.e., Korea) an independent state. The modern Joseon system that he advocated, especially the Gospel work, continued and greatly developed without him.

As in other countries, evangelical work in Korea has been accomplished through the dedication of foreign missionaries and active acceptance and spread of the Gospel by the Koreans. Therefore, I will give a brief overview of how Koreans have actively received and spread the Gospel.

In August 1872, the Scottish Presbyterian Church sent Williamson to Shandong, China, as a missionary. He was followed by John Ross and John MacIntyre. The latter two changed their mission field to Goryeomun(고려문), Tonghua, Manchuria, the northern province of China. The city of Tonghua was the gateway for trade between the Qing Dynasty(China) and Joseon(Korea), allowing them to meet many Koreans there.

Jian(集安, 지안) was one part of Tonghua(通化, 통화) in Jilin Province(吉林省, 길림성), where John Ross and John MacIntyre prepared for the Korean mission.

Sorae Church(소래 교회) was the first church in Korea.

At the time, Daewongun's isolation policy prevented Westerners from entering Joseon. Thus, the two decided to translate the Bible for Koreans. They then met a man named Eung-Chan Lee(이응찬), learned Korean from him, published the Korean textbook "Corean Print," translated the Bible into Korean with the help of Hong-Jun Bae(배홍준), Jin-Gi Kim(김진기), and Seong-Ha Lee(이성하), and baptized these three individuals.

Meanwhile, Su-Jeong Lee(이수정) was baptized in Japan on April 29, 1883, and wrote Nongjeongshinpyeon(농정신편, 農政新編) to introduce Christianity.

Sorae Church(소래 교회), the first church in Korea, was established in 1883 in Sorae, Daegu-myeon, Jangyeon-gun, Hwanghae-do(황해도 장연군 대구면 솔내). That was a year before Allen entered Joseon.

Sang-Ryun Seo(서상륜, 1848-1926), born in Ui-Ju(의주), the border town between Korea and China, traveled to Manchuria(that is, the northern province of China) to sell ginseng. However, his business efforts failed, and he became infected with typhus, which put him in danger of death. He was healed with the help of Scottish Presbyterian missionaries Pastor Ross and MacIntyre. Upon rising from his sickbed, he and his brother Kyung-Jo Seo(서경조) became believers and helped Pastor Ross translate the Bible into Korean and staying with him until the publication was finished.

In October 1882, when Sang-Ryun Seo came to Korea with Protestant brochures and a Korean Bible, he was arrested by the Korean police and imprisoned. However, he fled and founded a church called "Sorae Church" in 1883 in his hometown of Sorae, Jangyeon-gun, Hwanghae-do(today: Sorae village in Gumi-ri, Ryongyeon-gun, Hwanghaenam-do, 현 황해도 룡견군 금리 소래마을), in a thatched-roof house. In his village, the two brothers of the Seo family diligently evangelized the people, so that the majority of the villagers became believers and attended church.

This Sorae Church played a prominent role in the early history of Korean Protestantism. An example of this is that when Underwood founded the Saemoonan Church in early 1887, 13 of 14 founding members were from the Sorae Church.

And Sang-Ryun Seo's younger brother, Kyung-Jo Seo(서경조), graduated from Pyongyang Presbyterian Seminary and was one of the first seven Koreans to be ordained as Protestant pastors.

If we study the early history of the Korean Protestant Church, we can see that God blessed the cooperation of foreign missionaries and Koreans in evangelizing Korea. We can all give glory to God.

Sorae Church: The first thatched church and the rebuilt church with roof tiles

Source: Incheonin.com(황해도 소래교회 - 한국 최초의 "자생교회") on April 26, 2012

5. Churches in My Hometown of Shinryewon

I would now like to introduce the churches in my hometown of Shinryewon. When I was in elementary and middle school, there was only one church, "Shinryewon Holiness Church"(신례원 성결교회), near the old "Shinryewon Three-Way Intersection"(신례원 삼거리). The Holiness Churches, which emerged from the Wesleyan movement, began their work in Korea in 1907 and were originally called "The Oriental Missionary Society"(동방선교회). The Shinryewon Holiness Church was founded in 1938 as a branch of the Sapgyo Holiness Church(삽교 성결교회, founded in 1923) and the Yesan-eup Holiness Church(예산 성결교회, founded in 1932). In 1943, all Holiness Churches in Korea were forcibly closed for refusing to worship Japanese shrines. After the liberation of Korea, the Shinryewon Holiness Church(신례원 성결교회) was reopened in October 1945, and a little later this church was built near the Yonggulcheon Railway Bridge(용굴천 철도다리), not far from the old Shinryewon Three-Way Intersection(신례원 삼거리). In October 1985, the church moved to the east side of Shinryewon Elementary School(신례원 초등학교).

My third and fourth sisters attended this Holiness Church until their marriage. My brother also attended this church and experienced great joy in faith. After my mother died in January 1979, my brother's family moved to Seoul.

God heard the prayers of my third and fourth sisters, who had prayed for me since I was in elementary school, and prepared my heart for the Gospel through my Christian friends. And God led me to believe in Jesus during my first year of university.

Shinryewon Holiness Church (신례원성결교회) and other churches in Shinryewon, my hometown

Shinryewon Holiness Church (신례원성결교회)

신례원초등학교(Shinryewon Elementary School)

Protestant Churches in Shinryewon

신례원성당 Catholic Church

저의 생가(My Birthhome), 신례원역(Shinryewon Railway Station),

According to the Christian Newspaper of July 5, 2006, on the Internet, the evangelization rate in Yesan-gun, my hometown, is about 25%, which is slightly higher than the 18.3% of all (evangelical) Christians in Korea.

Fourth Story: In Germany, Esther becomes a Child of God and radiates Joy

"And Mary said: 'My soul glorifies the Lord and my spirit rejoices in God my Savior'" (Luke 1: 46-47)

1. Esther Comes to West Germany as a Nurse's Aide

Esther in her room in the nurses' house of Witten Hospital in 1971

Esther had been a happy child. But after she was sent back home from school during class in the second semester of the first year of middle school because she had not paid her school fees on time, she was deeply wounded in her heart. She was desperate about her fate of being born into a poor family. In her testimony of faith at the Summer Bible Conference in Seewis, Switzerland, in September 1974, she said the following:

> I grew up as the youngest of three children in a poor farming family. My brother and I are 14 years apart, and I was the beloved child of the family because I was the youngest. I was able to attend middle school even though our family was poor.
>
> When I was in the second semester of my first year of middle school, I was sent back home during class because I couldn't pay the school fee on time. After that, I had no joy in going to school; I lost motivation to study. I always thought to myself, "Why was I born into a poor family? Should I continue to go to school despite the contempt?" I had no joy and was full of dissatisfaction. Of course, I couldn't go to high school, and I secretly shed many tears.
>
> I had learned a song during music class in the fourth year of elementary school that had motivated me to become a nurse:
>
> "On the battlefield where bullets fly,
> A nurse in a nursing cap
> taking care of people who are bleeding.
> You are holy like an angel!"

My wish was to become a nurse and care for patients. But I wasn't allowed to go to high school.(So I couldn't go to nursing school.) The gap between my dream and my reality was so great that I was in great pain.

I started blaming poverty, society, and even my parents for it:

"If you can't send me to school, why did you give birth to me?"

With such words, I hurt my mother every day. My mom and I wept together.

But I shouldn't just cry. Since I lived in a poor farming family, I had to help out with all the work, from sowing to harvest. I thought, "Yes, let's work hard to overcome poverty."

I worked as hard as I could. Likewise, I also worked as a salesperson for 'the Agricultural Cooperative,' as a nanny in a daycare center, sewing and knitting. But I couldn't open a knitting shop(due to lack of money). So I worked in a doctor's office as a doctor's assistant(without professional training).

One day, after I had been working there for about a year and a half, I read an article in a newspaper ad entitled "Employment of Nurse's Aide(in West Germany)."

"Yes, I can fly to West Germany and work there as a nurse's aide!" I decided to leave the doctor's office, persuaded my parents, and attended 9 months of vocational training as a nurse's aide. After my training, I left my parents, who were stubbornly against my flight to West Germany, and came to West Germany in 1970.

Esther attended a nurse's aide course in Gwangju for about 9 months - from March 5 to December 12, 1969 - and became a nurse's aide. On August 8, 1970, she flew from Korea to West

Germany. In 1970, Korea was still an underdeveloped country, and the salaries of most professions were very low compared to the salaries in Germany. The monthly salary of a nurse's aide in West Germany in 1970 was around 600 marks, which was a high sum for a Korean woman.

Esther came to Germany and thought she could be happy if she had enough money so that her family members in Korea could go to the hospital if needed and live happily without asking anyone to lend them money.

After arriving in Germany, she had to work in the Evangelical Hospital in Witten, a neighboring city of Bochum, from August 19, even though she had only learned simple German in Korea for two weeks. That's why she had to learn German and medical terminology at work.

She also had to fight against the loneliness because of the foreign German culture. She sent the most of her salary to her family members in Korea. But money didn't make her happy; she was lonely and sad.

2. Esther believes in the Gospel and is full of Joy

Around 1964, Esther attended a sewing course in her hometown of Jangheung, which was run by Mrs. Jung-Hi Park(박정희). Jung-Hi Park was the wife of Pastor Nam-Young Jeong(정남영) of the Jangheung Church. At the invitation of Jung-Hi Park, Esther visited her church once or twice. Esther helped Mrs. Jung-

Hi Park during her difficult delivery of her youngest daughter, for which Jung-Hi Park was grateful. When Esther came to Germany, Jung-Hi Park asked her younger sister, Ok-Hi Park(박옥희), who had come to Germany in 1960 as a nursing student, to help Esther find faith in Jesus.

Thus, in 1970, Ok-Hi Park began mailing Esther "Daily Bread" booklets(a daily Bible reading guide) from the University Bible Fellowship in Korea. In early 1973, Ok-Hi Park visited Esther and subsequently invited her to the Bible conference in the Baptist Church in Witten/Ruhr, a city right next to Bochum, which took place from December 29, 1973, to January 5, 1974. During the conference, 19 Korean nurses, including Esther, presented their testimonies of faith. On January 5, 1974, these 19 nurses were baptized by Pastor Eikel, a Baptist minister.

Those baptized were Hye-Kyung Choi, Su-Ja Noh, Esther Hwang, Yang-Rim Hwang, Young-Hee Oh, Esther Choe(Note from Ok-Hi Park: 2. Sam 7, Daily Bread of Nov. 26: "God sees the heart of a person"), Young-Ja Park, Kwang-Ja Oh, Gyeong-Rye Kim, Jong-Rim Park, Young-Sir Kim, Byeong-Suk Lim, Chun-Hee Jeong, Ye-Ja Kim, Ok-Hwa Jeong, Kyeong-Ja Kim, Ok-Soon Choi, and Gil-Ja Lee.

Happy Esther after her new birth.

This photo was taken during the excursion of the missionaries in the Netherlands on June 3, 1974.

In 1974, Esther worked at the General Hospital in Hagen, and she studied Genesis in February 1974 with Ki-Hyang Lee(이기향), because Lee worked at the Bergmannsheil Hospital in Bochum, the closest to Hagen.

When Esther visited Korea in late April 1974, she studied the Bible in the Jongno UBF Center in Seoul from May 3 to 28, 1974. She was subsequently called as a missionary and returned to West Germany. When she was called as a missionary, she presented her testimony of faith entitled "God has called me, a sinner".

After her trip to Korea, she studied the Bible with Ki-Hyang Lee, particularly the book of Romans and the Gospel of John.

During the West German Summer Conference in Seewis, Switzerland, on September 16-22, 1974, Esther deeply received God's Word, John 1:4, through the sermon of Chang-Woo Lee(이창우) entitled "The Light of the People." She later confessed that through this word she had personally accepted Jesus.

Esther began helping Korean nurses such as Soo-Hyeon Kim(김수현), Kyung-Sun Moon(문경순), Soo-Yeon Kim(김수연), Bu-Young Kim(김부영), Ok-Hee Kim(김옥희), and Kyung-Sook Oh(오경숙) with Bible study.

In 1976, she moved to the Evangelical Hospital in Rheda-Wiedenbrück and helped Korean and German nurses in Rheda and other cities with Bible studies.

The hospitals where Esther worked:

Aug 19, 1970 - July 31, 1973: Evangelical Hospital in Witten
Jun 30, 1973 - Jun 30, 1976: General Hospital in Hagen.
Jul 1, 1976 - Mar 31, 1978: Evangelical Hospital in Rheda-Wiedenbrück
Apr 1, 1978 - Apr 10, 1979: Evangelical Nursing Home in Schwerte
Work break for 8 months to look after baby Stephan
Jan 1, 1980 - Aug 31, 1991: Bethanien Evangelical Hospital in Dortmund-Hörde
Sep 1, 1991 - Aug 31, 2009: Elisabeth Hospital in Bochum
*** Early retirement from Sep. 1, 2009

Fifth Story: My Rebirth and My Joyful Life during University

"The Word became flesh and made his dwelling among us. We have seen his glory, the glory of the one and only Son, who came from the Father, full of grace and truth." (John 1:14)

1. My New Life in Daejeon, Korea

⋆ Enrollment at the University

In February 1970, I went to the university treasury to pay the entrance tuition fee and enroll in the university. At that time, I had received a scholarship of 30,000 won(about 100 dollars) from Yesan High School and another 30,000 won from the Technical College of Chungnam University. The total tuition was around 30,000 won. So I had about 30,000 won more than the tuition fee. In front of me was Y.-J. Kim, who wanted to enroll in the English literary faculty. She asked the cashier if it was possible for her to pay the tuition fee about a week later. But the cashier, an old man, replied, "No." So I offered to lend her my money. The cashier recommended that she bring the money to him after a week so that he could return the money to me. A week later, I got my money back. I'm not the type of person willing to help others, but God gave me the grace to receive double scholarships from the high school and the college, and God also gave me the heart to lend her the money as I stood right behind her and overheard their conversation.

⋆ A Room for Me and Yong-Seong Seo at the Orphanage in Daejeon

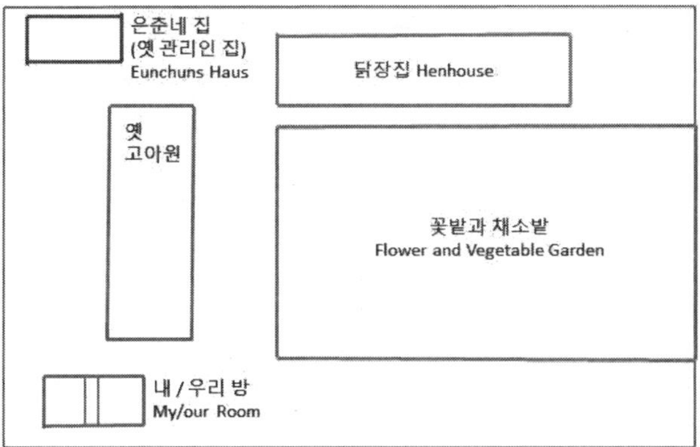

Eun-Chun's house and my room(92 Gayang-dong, Jung-gu, Daejeon)

If a village student wanted to go to university in a big city like Daejeon, he had to solve two financial problems: tuition fees and room rent. The scholarship I received at the time was roughly equivalent to the tuition fees. But that could leave the room issue unsolved because my family couldn't pay the rent for my room in Daejeon. Thank God my friend's family from his hometown moved to Daejeon around December 1969.

Eun-Chun Lee's uncle, a Catholic priest, was the head of Mary's Hospital in Daejeon at that time. Eun-Chun Lee's parents signed a lease with the Catholic Church for a former orphanage and moved there as the caretakers of the vacant orphanage in Gayang-dong, Jung-gu, Daejeon. The orphanage had housed orphans orphaned by the Korean War from 1950 to 1953. There was a house for the caretaker's family, a building with many rooms for orphans, and a small apartment with two separate rooms. Eun-Chun's parents gave me a room in the small apartment, and I shared it with my hometown friend Yong-Seong Seo, who also attended Chungnam National University. Eun-Chun's parents were Catholics who believed in God and were merciful. My mother brought me rice and side dishes such as potatoes, red chili paste (gochujang), and soybean paste. I thank God for me through my mother, brother, and family.

Yong-Seong Seo, who shared the room with me, attended the Physics Department at Chungnam National University. In addition to studying physics, he also worked diligently to pass a state examination of law. If he passed the state examination of law, he would become a public prosecutor, judge, or lawyer. At my invitation, Yong-Seong Seo attended Bible studies in our church a few times. Unfortunately, he stopped attending our church. He met a woman student, married her after graduating, and was then called to military service. I later heard that he died in an accident in the military. How sad were his parents and brothers and sisters! And how would the newly married woman have felt? May God comfort his parents, brothers, and sisters, especially his young wife, and give them eternal life through faith in Jesus Christ.

⋆ **Bok-Nam Ha**

After living with me for two years, Yong-Seong Seo moved into a rented apartment near Chungnam National University. And Bok-Nam Ha(하복남), my sister-in-law's youngest brother, moved into my room. He was about seven years younger than I. He graduated from Yesan Middle School and then attended Daejeon Technical School for five years of professional training.

In general, I came home late from our church. I'm sorry I didn't pay much attention to Bok-Nam at the time. However, God took care of him and led him to YFC(Youth for Christ), a Christian youth group. The founder of this group was Pastor Billy Kim(Korean name: Jang-Hwan Kim, 김장환) of the Baptist Church. Bok-Nam Ha became a faithful Christian through this group. He also studied well at the school and became a good electrician after graduation. He faithfully served the Lord at Daeheung Baptist Church(대흥 침례교회) in Daejeon, married a woman of faith, and lived a happy married life. God answered the prayers of my third and fourth sisters and of Bok-Nam. Bok-Nam had a good influence on my sister-in-law and her siblings, so that my sister-in-law and her sister became Christians.

I thank God that He gave me and Bok-Nam Ha a room in Daejeon for free through Eun-Chun Lee's parents and led us to believe in Jesus Christ. God's providence is mysterious and very good.

⋆ University Entrance Ceremony

The entrance ceremony of the Chungnam National University was held on March 2, 1970. All 580 new students gathered department by department at the university sports complex in Munhwa-dong, Daejeon(대전시 문화동), as the professors stood in front of them. The university president congratulated us on joining the university. As the freshman representative, I appeared before the students and read the Freshman Manifesto(신입생 선서). The content of this freshman manifesto was, I think, that we(i.e., the freshmen) would adhere to the university's rules and concentrate on our studies. Through this ceremony, I became known to all freshmen and many professors because I was limping. I believe that at this ceremony, God made me known as a blessing to all students and the world.

The word "university" originally comes from the Latin "universus," which means "the whole world." In the past, I hadn't been interested in all of Korea or the whole world, but only in my little world. Because I had thought that it would be too far for me, as a poor person, to think about all of Korea or the whole world. But God called me to be a person who looks to the world and brings them the good news of blessing.

That same year, God took another important step in His work: He sent Esther to Germany. Of course, I didn't know God's plan at that time. Just as starting university was a significant step for me to be a blessing to the world, Esther's arrival in Germany was a big leap for her to be a blessing to Germany and the world.

God had a wonderful plan for me and Esther, and His puzzle gradually fell into place over the years.

⋆ My Fellow Students

I chose chemical engineering as my major. Law or economics deals with interpersonal relationships, for example, as a prosecutor or businessman. With a job like that, I didn't believe I could be honest in such a profession. I opted for engineering, especially chemical engineering, because I considered the chances of getting a job for people with a science degree to be worse than for those with an engineering degree. God was working in secret, and so I chose chemical engineering as my subject, married Esther after graduation, and came to Germany as a student missionary with the help of Professor Bo-Sung Rhee(이보성 교수) from the chemical engineering department.

There were 40 students in my department. At that time, students attended lectures by department. This created a friendship among the fellow students of the same department. Most of our fellow students were from Chungnam High School or Daejeon High School in Daejeon. The rest came from Gongju High School(공주 사대부고) or other high schools. The department spokesman was elected at the beginning of the first semester. Most of the colleagues in my department were from Chungnam High School(충남 고등학교). Thus, Yoon-Gi Choi(최윤기), a graduate of Chungnam High School, became the spokesman. He had a cheerful, sociable, and considerate character that made him well-suited for the department spokesman. After graduating, he proved his leadership skills in his company, so that he was promoted to managing director. Jong-Chan Sim(심종찬) also visited our church for a while. I believe that God has blessed him. In the sophomore or junior year, Hwan-Young Kim(김환영), a graduate of Daejeon High School, took over as the spokesperson for the department. He was a friendly, calm, and loyal fellow student, and he was a diligent researcher. He met a student in the nursing department and married her after completing his master's thesis. I later found out that she was a Christian. I believe that God led Hwan-Young Kim and his children to faith and richly blessed his family.

Some of my colleagues in the department, such as Jae-Cheon Yoo(유재천, graduated a year later than we), Soo-Young Kim(김수영), Jun-Taek Sim(심준택), and Jin-Woong Kim(김진웅), were Christians when they began their studies.

Jin-Woong Kim was calm, and he had believed in Christ from a young age, so his belief did not waver. He visited our student church for a while. I had a good relationship with him, and I really appreciate his friendship. Jun-Taek graduated from the high school affiliated with Gongju National University of Education. He was active and cheerful. Dae-Young Choi(최대영), a Daejeon High School graduate, visited our church for a while at my invitation and also attended a conference. I miss his friendly face. Soo-Young Kim was a bright and happy friend. He attended our service for a while.

Ho Kang(강호), a graduate of Daejeon High School, was a very cheerful friend, but he drank alcohol. He was active in the

UNESCO group. He was not a Christian at the time, but at the invitation of Eun-Kyung Ahn(안은경), a member of UNESCO, he had studied the Bible with her for a while in our church. After graduating from university, he became a military officer. After I resigned from my position as a research assistant in the Department of Chemical Engineering at Chungnam University on March 1, 1977, Ho Kang became an assistant there and married Ki-Nam Lee(이기남). After completing his master's degree, he and his wife flew to the United States, where he earned his doctorate. There, he was invited by one of his predecessors from Daejeon High School to study the Bible. After studying the Bible, he came home, and when he took a sip of alcohol, he felt like the alcohol was burning in him. From that day on, he stopped drinking. So he experienced a dramatic conversion like Saul to Paul. After completing his doctorate in the United States, he visited me in Bochum, Germany, and told me about his dramatic conversion.

Shortly after visiting me, he was appointed a professor in the newly established Environmental Engineering Department at Chungnam National University. He invited Pastor Dong-Myeong Kim(김동명), the husband of Yi-Suk Ahn(안이숙), who is the author of the book "If I Die, I Die"(죽으면 죽으리라), from the USA and founded a new church in the Daedeok research complex. Many PhDs from the research complex attend Sunday worship at this church. As a professor, Ho Kang eagerly taught students. He also researched diligently and published the research results in specialist journals. He attended the theological seminary in the evening and was ordained a pastor. He is actively involved in missions in neighboring countries and Africa.

Myung-Hee Han(한명희) started his studies three years earlier than I did. After completing his military service, he returned to university and attended lectures with us. I invited him to a Bible study, and he came to believe in the Gospel. He married Young-Seo Kim(김영서), who had worked as a missionary in Germany. After the marriage, he and his wife were sent to Chicago, USA, as lay missionaries.

2. My Grateful Professors

⋆ Byung-Woo Kim(김병우), Philosophy Professor

In their first year of study, students took many liberal arts courses in their freshman year. To this end, a classroom building was constructed and named the Faculty of Liberal Arts. The liberal arts subjects included Korean, English, ethics, philosophy, world cultural history, a second foreign language, physical education, and military training.

Professor Byung-Woo Kim taught philosophy in our department. He lectured on the French philosopher Descartes and explained how Descartes could believe in the existence of God.

Descartes initially doubted everything. He also doubted the existence of God. However, he couldn't doubt that there was an

"I" who doubted the existence of God. Ironically, his doubting God was evidence of God's existence.

Through this lecture, Professor Kim aimed to help students believe in God. He advised students that if someone gave them a Bible, they should not throw it away but read it.

At that time, my faith was still in its early stages. Around May 1970, after the philosophy class, I entered into Professor Byung-Woo Kim's room and asked him how one could believe the miracle stories in the Bible. He answered me, "The miracle stories in the Bible are there for us to believe in Jesus." Surprisingly, his explanation resolved my question. Since then, I have not felt any contradiction between the biblical stories and my scientific thinking.

For some reason, I felt that he must be the son of the famous Korean poet Dong-Myeong Kim(김동명). I had learned about the poet Dong-Myeong Kim from the history of Korean literature while preparing for the university entrance exam. When I asked the professor if he was the son of the poet Dong-Myeong Kim, he replied, "Yes." He said that his father was a Protestant and he was a Catholic. When I asked him why he became a Catholic when his father was a Protestant, he replied that the Catholic Church was the mainstream of Christianity. I didn't ask him further. It didn't matter to me whether someone was a Protestant Christian or a Catholic Christian. The only important thing for me was that one genuinely believed in Jesus Christ.

Dong-Myeong Kim(1901-1968) studied theology at Aoyama-Gakuin University in Japan during the Japanese colonial period and then worked as a poet in Korea. He refused to change his Korean name to Japanese, moved to the country, and wrote poetry. After Korea's liberation from Japan, he became a professor at Ewha University(이화 대학교) in Seoul.

About two years later, I saw Professor Byung-Woo Kim come to our student church and humbly learn the book of Genesis from Eun-Kyung Ahn, an English student.

I asked him how he, a philosophy professor, could humbly learn God's word from her.

He answered me, "I am a student."

I later heard that he had switched to Hannam University(한남 대학교, a Protestant university).

⋆ Sports Professor Chang-Gi Min(민창기), Korean Professor Jae-Dong Sa(사재동), English Professor Young-Eui Park(박영의)

God also encouraged me through sports professor Chang-Gi Min. He shared my entrance exam results with Allen during our physical education class. Perhaps he had graded the applicant's examination papers and therefore knew my exam results. At the end of the semester, he gave me an A grade(top grade) and explained in front of all fellow students why he had given me an A grade: because I had actively participated in practical physical education. His yardstick was revolutionary. At that time, most professors gave students the grades as a comparison with other students. I was greatly encouraged by his explanation.

At the Korean lecture, Professor Jae-Dong Sa lectured on his research results on ancient folk songs in the Chungcheong-do region. His opinion was different from the conventional views. He praised drinking alcohol during the lecture. I searched the internet and found that, being a devout Buddhist, he wanted to become a Buddhist monk. I believe that God's blessings rest on him and his descendants.

Professor Young-Eui Park taught us English in our first year of university. He was very kind to me. When I later showed him my master's thesis, "A Study on Pyrolysis of Oak Trees," which I had written in English and submitted without correction by others, and had already passed, he told me that if I had shown him the work prior to submitting it, he could have corrected the work linguistically. I still remember his warm encouragement.

⋆ Professors of My Chemical Engineering Department

Before moving to Youseong(유성), Chungnam National University(except for the Faculty of Medicine) was located in Munhwa-dong, Daejeon. The Faculty of Medicine and the University Hospital are now located at the former site of the Faculty of Humanities and Sciences in Munhwa-dong. During my studies, the university had not yet moved to Youseong. After four years of study, I worked as a research assistant, assisting Mr. Hyuk-Jong Joo in preparing the documents for transporting the faculty's experimental equipment to Youseong.

During my time as a research assistant, Professor Hong-Bin

Lim, a graduate of Gyeonggi High School(경기 고등학교) and Seoul National University, was the dean. He was very friendly; one could therefore call him an international gentleman.

Professor Won-Pyo Hong(홍원표) taught industrial chemistry and helped students find jobs after graduation.

Professor Jin-Seon Kim(김진선) taught inorganic chemistry and worked in academic administration at the university's central office. Sadly, he passed away while I was still a research assistant.

Professor Ki-Seok Maeng(맹기석) was a polymer expert who had returned from his doctoral studies at McGill University in Canada to teach us organic chemistry and polymer engineering.

Professor Bo-Sung Rhee(이보성), a graduate of Yonsei University(연세 대학교), received his doctorate from the University of Karlsruhe. He taught us thermodynamics and unit engineering. He was my master's thesis supervisor. I will write more about him later.

Professor Hong-Sik Choi(최홍식) was one of the first graduates of the Department of Chemical Engineering at Chungnam National University. He taught us chemistry and physical chemistry during my first year of study and tried not to miss a single lecture. He also diligently conducted experimental research. During my doctoral studies in Dortmund, he conducted research at the University of Dortmund for a year. Although he was still young, he died during my doctoral studies in Dortmund.

Hyuk-Jong Joo(주혁종) had earned his bachelor's degree three or four years earlier than I had. During my studies and work as a research assistant in Korea, he had worked as an assistant. He was like a kind older brother to me. When I came to Germany to study in January 1978, he was doing experimental research at the University of Dortmund. I met him on January 2, 1978, in the Department of Chemical Engineering at the University of Dortmund. He, Esther, and I read the Bible together and prayed to God that God would bless the entire university. At that time, he did not yet believe in Jesus. After this research, he returned to Korea and became a professor in the Department of Polymer Engineering at Chungnam National University.

3. From My New Birth to My Baptism

*** My Spiritual Tree-Planting Day: April 5, 1970**

The freshman admission ceremony was held on Monday, March 2, 1970, at the university stadium. After this ceremony, I went to the university library on the hill. On this hill, Peter Suh(서 베드로), the director of Daejeon UBF(now Daejeon CMI), spoke to me. He told me he knew me because Mr. Soo-Min Lee had told him about me. Soo-Min Lee was the German teacher at Yesan High School. And Peter Suh invited me to the UBF, but I replied, "Excuse me, I don't have time for that!" and I went into the library. At that time, I was determined to concentrate only on my studies. About a month has passed since then. At the time, Koreans had cut down trees from mountains and used them as firewood to cook rice and heat the rooms, leaving most mountains bare and treeless. Therefore, the government declared April 5th Tree-Planting Day and encouraged tree-planting. That year, Tree-Planting Day fell on a Sunday. I went to the university around 9 a.m. with a hoe because the university administration had invited students to plant trees. I watched as some trees were planted behind the library. Afterwards, I was on my way to the library when I met Peter Suh again. This time, Mr. Soo-Min Lee was also there.

After graduating from Hannam University(한남 대학교, then Daejeon College, 대전 대학), Mr. Lee worked as a teacher at Yesan High School and began a master's degree in chemical engineering at Chungnam National University under Professor Ki-Seok Maeng. Out of courtesy, I asked Soo-Min Lee where I could meet him in person. He replied that we could meet at the UBF student church at 3 p.m. At that time, the UBF student church in Daejeon held a service on Sunday at 3 p.m. So I went to the UBF student church to meet Soo-Min Lee.

The church was located near the east fence of Daejeon High School. Everyone in the church was friendly to me. Peter Suh preached in a calm voice, without shouting, so that his sermon didn't bother me. At the end of the service, everyone prayed in pairs. I was to pray with Kyoung-Sook Cho, a sophomore at Daejeon Nursing School(대전 간호학교). She kindly explained to me how to pray:

"At the beginning of the prayer, you say 'God' or 'Dear God' to address God. Then you name the concerns for which you would like to ask God for help or for which you are grateful. And because you can only come to God through Jesus Christ, at the end of the prayer you say, 'I pray in the name of Jesus Christ. Amen!' With that, the prayer ends."

Through her kind explanation, I was able to pray to God for the first time in my life. That was the beginning of my faith in God and Jesus Christ. That's why I call the day my "Spiritual Tree-Planting Day."

⋆ Believed in Jesus as God Incarnate through John 1:1 + 14: April 6, 1970

After Sunday worship(on the same day), Peter Suh invited me to the English conversation course, which was held at the church on weekday evenings. Although I had already learned a lot of English, my pronunciation wasn't good. I wanted to improve my pronunciation and began attending the evening English conversation course regularly.

We first practiced English pronunciation for about 30 minutes, then learned the Gospel of John in Korean. On the first day, we studied John 1:1-18. Surprisingly, John 1:1 and 1:14 helped me believe that Jesus was originally God and that he came to earth as a human being.

John 1:1, "In the beginning was the Word, and the Word was with God, and the Word was God."

John 1:14, "The Word became flesh and made his dwelling

among us. We have seen his glory, the glory of the one and only Son, who came from the Father, full of grace and truth."

This discovery seemed nothing special, yet it was an important event in my life. After serious discussions with my Catholic friend Jae-Beom Lee during my middle school years about how to know the existence of God, I had come to the conclusion that I could prove neither the existence nor the non-existence of God. Now, in the first chapter of the Gospel of John, I found the correct answer to the question of God's existence.

*** Experienced Great Joy at the Bulkwangdong Bible Conference in Seoul: Mid-May 1970**

In mid-May, Eun-Chun Lee, a friend from my hometown, was supposed to be drafted into the military. His family had given me a room for free. So, I planned a farewell party for him on the weekend with my roommate Yong-Seong Seo. However, Peter Suh suggested that I attend the spring student conference in Seoul as a guest with Young-Ja Kwon from Daejeon College. I asked Eun-Chun Lee for his understanding and attended the conference, which was held at a conference center in Bulgwang-dong, Eunpyeong-dong, Seoul. It was a very unfortunate decision for my friend Eun-Chun Lee.

Most of the participants in this conference were Seoul National University students from Jongno UBF. Everyone was friendly and cheerful. Kang-Bok Lee(이강복, now Abraham Lee in Cologne), then a second-year student at Seoul National

University, was also there and was very kind to me. On April 5th and 6th of that same year, I had believed in Jesus intellectually. But during this conference, through their kindness and the work of the Holy Spirit, God opened my heart, so I believed in Jesus with great joy.

Until the conference, I had not attended Sunday worship. But after the conference in Seoul, I began to attend Sunday worship in Daejeon with joy. I also willingly attended the Spring Conference of the Student Church of Daejeon in June in Maepo (매포), a suburb of Daejeon.

⋆ Change from Self-Centered Faith to God-Centered Faith: Summer Bible School in late July 1970

The university's summer vacation began around July 10th of that year. I planned to spend the summer vacation in my home village and study intensively on Mount Yonggol(용골산), similar to my preparation for the university entrance exam. However, Peter Suh suggested I stay in Daejeon and learn English in the weekly TIME magazine course.

After studying English with the TIME for about a week, missionary Sarah Barry from Seoul came as a preacher and taught for a week at a Bible school, where she taught us the Acts of the Apostles. Each day, we were required to answer the Bible text questionnaire individually, study it together as a group, and then listen to Sarah Barry's sermon. Afterwards, everyone was to write down their personal opinion on the text and share it with the group the next day. I had to sacrifice my entire day and week just for this Bible school. I hadn't imagined it would take so much time.

I had a strong feeling of wasting time, and one day tears came down my face. But with these tears, my heart opened wide to the world of the Holy Spirit. And I experienced God's great love for me and felt great joy. It was the personal experience that transformed me from an egocentric person to a God-centered person.

On April 5th and 6th, God helped me to accept Jesus as the Son of God according to my understanding. Then He helped me experience great emotional joy during the spring conference in Seoul. Finally, in the Summer Bible School, God transformed me from a self-centered person to a God-centered person and filled my heart to the fullest with the joy of the Kingdom of God.

⋆ Summer Bible Conference: Early August 1970

At the beginning of August, the Summer Bible Conference was held at Soongsil University(숭실 대학교) in Seoul. Because I had experienced great joy through the Summer Bible School, I invited my fellow students to this conference. One of my classmates, Dae-Young Choi(최대영), a graduate of Daejeon High School, attended. He was a person with a warm heart for others. God blessed him and his family. I also invited Gu-Hee Jung(정구희), a student of the nursing department and a graduate of Yesan Girls' High School, and she attended.

Nam-Sik Woo(우남식) came from Dangjin, a neighboring town of Yesan. Like me, he started visiting our student church in March or April 1970. Until then, he knew neither Jesus Christ nor Christianity. But he became a Christian through Bible study, and he was so joyful in God's blessings. Out of joy in Jesus, he invited many fellow students in his department to study the Bible. According to my list of attendees at the 1970 Summer Conference, his department colleagues Han-Woo Lee(이한우), Sang-Do Hwang(황상도), and Jong-Jin Park(박종진) attended the conference.

⋆ Joy of the Earthly Paradise

In the spring semester of 1970, I was richly blessed by God so that my eyes were opened step by step to the spiritual world, and I became a completely new person in the Lord Jesus. I experienced great joy because of God's great love for me. Faith in Jesus Christ gave me a whole new perspective on the world. I felt the world around the university campus was a paradise; walking around the campus made me feel like I was walking in paradise. I realized that students who did not yet believe in Jesus Christ were in dire need of the Gospel of salvation and God's blessing. So, around June 1970, I started inviting students to worship in our church. After the summer vacation, I invited the students more eagerly than before.

First, I invited students from our department. There were 40 students in our chemical engineering department. About half of them had once invited to our church. I came from a small village, which was why I only knew a few students personally, apart from those in our department. So, I got a list of all freshmen of the year. From the list, I learned that Gu-Hee Jung from the nursing department was a graduate of Yesan Girls' High School, my hometown. I bravely entered the lecture hall of the nursing department and invited Gu-Hee Jung to our church. She came and visited our church for about a year and believed in Jesus.

During the 1970-71 winter vacation, we studied the first book of the Bible, Genesis. In the first chapter of Genesis, it is reported that after creating all of creation, God also created humans. God looked at His creatures and people and said, "It is very good(or beautiful)!"(Genesis 1:31). Because God made each of us so beautiful and good and because He values us so much, all human beings have absolutely good meaning and precious value in God's eyes. Even if someone is injured in the body and looks a little unnatural, there is absolutely no reason to feel inferior, because God made him very beautiful and said that he is very good.

My right leg was injured, and I limped. That's why I had a complex. Through God's Word in Genesis 1:31, I realized that I was very beautiful and precious in God. This Word of the Bible freed me from my sense of inferiority and gave me indescribable joy.

Furthermore, Joseph's story in Genesis taught me that God had set my life on the best path. If my leg hadn't been injured, I could have finished elementary school two years earlier. If so, then I would have had to work as a farmer or lumberjack after elementary school and would have had no chance of attending middle school. In the 1960s, about 90% of Korea's population were farmers. Back then, the poor had little chance of finding a job other than as a farmer or a lumberjack. At the end of second grade of elementary school, I injured my right leg and missed four years of school. When I got back into fifth and sixth grades four years later, I was two years behind my peers. Because of this delay, I was assigned to have Mr. So-Hee Yeon as my class teacher in the 6th grade. Amid my family's poverty, he helped me get a scholarship to go to middle school. After graduating from middle school, I attended Yesan Agricultural School for two years. After two years, I moved to the third grade of Yesan High School and was one of the first graduates from Yesan High School. Yesan High School principal Seung-Tak Baek waived my tuition fee and promised me a scholarship to the university. Without this promise, I wouldn't have dared to go to university.

Above all, I cannot forget God's help through my mother, brother, and sisters. Even though my family was poor, they all raised and supported me with love and dedication.

God has also encouraged me through the kindness of friends like Yeon-Soo Park, Jae-Beom Lee, and Eun-Chun Lee.

Through Su-Min Lee, Peter Suh, and Kyoung-Sook Cho, God helped me believe in Jesus.

I thank all professors in the Chemical Engineering

Department, especially Prof. Bo-Sung Rhee, who supervised my master's thesis, for his help and kindness.

I also thank all my fellow students in the Chemical Engineering Department.

God has mobilized so many people to save and bless me.

Of course, that doesn't mean that my salvation has made me a superman who doesn't worry after believing in Jesus. I am still an ordinary person. I sometimes couldn't believe in God's care and worried about my future. But because God helped me renew my faith in His providence, I am able to move forward courageously and with great joy and confidence.

Everyone who has accepted and trusts Jesus can enjoy this kind of joy. Therefore, the Gospel is good news for all who believe in it. But, of course, God helps everyone differently. For example, God sent Esther, who would become my wife, to Germany as a nurse's aide when she was unable to go to high school after graduating from middle school due to her family's financial situation. And God led her to believe in Jesus in Germany and marry me.

There are many ways God can help us, the fundamental truth remains the same: God has made everyone very good and loves everyone very much. And God wants to give everyone eternal life and a happy life.

⋆ My Baptism: Summer 1971

Our student church's Sunday worship took place at 3 a.m. So every Sunday morning, I attended the Sunday worship of Daeheung Baptist Church(대흥 침례교회) near our student church with Peter Suh. Back then, our student church didn't baptize anyone. In the summer of 1971, I attended Pastor Jong-Man Ahn's preparatory course(안종만 목사) for baptism at Daeheung Baptist Church two or three times.

He asked me which Word of the Bible had convinced me that I had been saved. I hadn't thought of that until then. But then, I remembered the verses from the first day of my Bible study in our student church and answered him, "John 1:1, 14, 18."

John 1:1, "In the beginning was the Word, and the Word was with God, and the Word was God."

Verse 14, "The Word became flesh and made his dwelling among us. We have seen his glory, the glory of the one and only Son, who came from the Father, full of grace and truth."

Verse 18, "No one has ever seen God, but the one and only Son, who is himself God and is in closest relationship with the Father, has made him known."

These three verses say that Jesus was originally God who became a man named Jesus and revealed God to us. These verses have stayed in my mind ever since. After this course, I was baptized on July 25, 1971. The pastor immersed me entirely in the water and straightened me up again. This baptism process shows that because of my sins, I died with Jesus and was resurrected with Jesus.

God baptized Esther on January 5, 1974, in the Baptist Church in Witten by Pastor Eickel and 18 other nursing missionaries. Through the baptism, God prepared Esther and me as a married couple from eternity to serve the Lord with one heart and spread the Gospel.

4. Happy and Blessed University Years (from Sophomore Year to Graduation)

⋆ Chungnam National University Students' Weekly Bible Study Group

At that time, there were two universities in Daejeon: Chungnam National University and Daejeon College(now Hannam University), as well as the Daejeon Nursing School. At the beginning of the fall semester of 1970/71, Peter Suh organized a weekly meeting (in Korean, "Yo-Hee, 요회") for the students of Chungnam National University, a second weekly meeting for the students of Daejeon College, and one for the students of the Nursing School. He appointed a student leader for each group. Thus, I became the leader of the student meeting for Chungnam University students. When the new semester of my second year began in March 1971, I actively started inviting students to Bible study and Sunday worship.

Nam-Sik Woo began attending church around the same time

as I did. He invited Yong-Dae Kim(김용대), who started college a year after Woo. I will say more about him later.

Hye-Min Seo(서혜민), a student at Daejeon College, told me about Young-Gee Yoon(윤영기), a law student at Chungnam University who was her classmate at Holston Girls' High School. So I went to her and invited her to our church. But she replied that she didn't have time. At that time, Do-Yeol Chung(정도열, Caleb Chung) from Daegu was staying at our church as a staff intern. So I visited her again with Do-Yeol Chung. Chung told her, "Everyone wants to be successful. Unfortunately, many people can't be successful because they don't spend their time according to the right priorities. So if you want to be successful, you have to live according to the right priorities."

This advice gave her insight. So she came to our church and learned Genesis from him. She experienced God's love and great joy and invited friends like Jang-Won Son(손장원), Seong-Ja Park (박성자), and Seok-Hee Choi(최석희) to our church.

Nam-Sik Woo and I came from the villages of Dangjin(당진) and Yesan. Our speech and behavior betrayed it. But we didn't notice it ourselves. Young-Gee Yoon(now Ruth Ahn), Seong-Ja Park, and Jang-Won Son(now Rebecca Han) came from Daejeon, a big city. They talked about us and laughed at our behavior and speech. Seong-Ja Park told me about it later.

Once or twice during my sophomore year, I attended Sunday worships at the church Jang-Won Son's mother attended. There, I saw someone praying in a language I didn't understand. Jang-

Won Son told me that he was praying in tongues. At the time, I knew nothing about praying in tongues

Jang-Won Son's mother was a devout, open-minded, and kind person. Jang-Won Son's father managed a bank branch. God blessed Jang-Won Son's mother's faith and prayer. Thus, her children grew up in faith from an early age. And later, her husband also believed in Jesus. Jang-Won Son's older brother, Jang-Gwon Son(손장권), studied at Korea University and worked there as a sociology professor. His wife worked in the passport department of the Ministry of Foreign Affairs in Seoul at the time. When I applied for a passport to Germany at the end of 1977, she helped me obtain it quickly. I thank her very much for her kind help. God began the work of blessing through Jang-Won Son's mother and continued the work of blessing through Jang-Won Han.

Seong-Ja Park(박성자) was the eldest daughter of her family and cared for others well; she worked well with others for the mission. After graduating from university, she married Yeol-Soo Lim(임열수) and devoted herself to the student church. Later, after studying with her husband at a seminary in the United States, she and her husband established a church in Seoul, where she served as an assistant pastor. Her husband, Yeol-Soo Lim, became the first president of an Evangelical Theological University in Korea.

Seok-Hee Choi began her studies at Chungnam University the same year I did, majoring in business administration. She was humble and helped several students, including Myung-Ja Kim(김명자) and Hyun-Sook Kim(김현숙). After graduating, she worked at the headquarters of the Korea Exchange Bank in Seoul.

Eun-Kyung(Maria) Ahn(안은경) helped others well without hurting them because she understood others' feelings well. She was also loyal. From the first day, she remained faithful to our church and served the Lord faithfully. In her kindness, she also invited Professor Byung-Woo Kim(김병우), a philosophy professor, and taught him Genesis. After graduating, she worked for a while as an English teacher. Since December 1977, she has served the Lord full-time in the church, married Nam-Sik Woo, and helped him well. After the wedding, the couple established a new student church in Incheon, helped the students with the Gospel, and sent many missionaries abroad.

Yong-Dae Kim was a gifted student. He graduated from Daejeon High School and attended the Naval Academy. However, he had to leave the academy to study at the Faculty of Technical Education at Chungnam University. He had a good understanding of others, which is why everyone liked him. Jeong-Hee Han(한정희) also liked him and later married him. Yong-Dae Kim retired after serving as a school principal. He is one of the two elders of the Daejeon Mission Church for All Nations and serves the church faithfully.

Jeong-Hee Han, his wife, understands others' feelings well and helps them. She also serves the church faithfully as an exhorter.

⋆ The Weekly Student Group from Chungnam National University's College of Medicine, College of Agriculture, and College of Law & Business

In the fall of 1970, our church began holding weekly meetings for the first time. Peter Suh, the church leader, appointed me as the leader of the student group at Chungnam University and Nam-Sik Woo as the head of the World Missions Department.

At the beginning of the fall semester of 1971-72, Peter Suh divided the Chungnam University Bible students into two weekly groups. He appointed Nam-Sik Woo as the leader of the student groups of Chungnam University College of Technology and the College of Humanities and Science. He also appointed me as the leader of the student groups of Chungnam University College of Medicine, the College of Agriculture, and the College of Law and Business Administration. Furthermore, he also appointed Jang-Won Son as the first co-worker for Nam-Sik Woo's group and Seok-Hee Choi for my group.

The reason for dividing the Chungnam University students into two groups was, of course, the large number of Bible students from Chungnam University. However, the following episode also played a role in this division.

At the beginning of the fall semester of 1971, Nam-Sik Woo and I met by chance in the corridor of our technical college. Nam-Sik Woo suggested appointing Yong-Dae Kim, who was studying the Bible with him, as the successor leader for the Chungnam University student group. I replied that In-Seop

Lim(임인섭), who was studying the Bible with me, should be the successor. When we couldn't agree, we began to pray together; he prayed that Yong-Dae Kim would be appointed as the group's successor, and I prayed that In-Seop Lim would be appointed. Later. Later, Yong-Dae became the group leader of Nam-Sik Woo's group, and In-Seop Lim became group leader of my group. This incident showed me how immature I was in my faith. But God used my immaturity to split one group into two, thus leading more students to faith.

In the spring of 1971, I taught the Bible to In-Seop Lim[2), a freshman from Agricultural College. He didn't believe in Jesus at the time. When he came to our church to study the Bible, he brought the Bible wrapped in newspaper so that other students could not see it. Sometimes, during a break in lectures, I went into his lecture hall and prayed with him when other students were there. He later told me that he was ashamed of his fellow students at the time.

However, after personally accepting Jesus as his Savior, he became courageous and actively invited other students to believe. He succeeded me as group leader and became an active student evangelist. As a result, he helped Joo-Yeon Kim(김주연), Gi-Sang Yoon(윤기상), Myung-Sook Yang(양명숙), and Soon-Ok Yoo(유순옥) believe in Jesus and live as disciples of Jesus.

After graduating from university, In-Seop Lim enlisted in the

---

2) In-Seop Lim: "Singing on the restroom"(Korean edition), Coram Deo, South Korea, 2000, S. 198-202.

military. Two or three months later, I met him at a highway rest stop. He explained that he had been unexpectedly discharged from military service. The people in his hometown had encouraged him to study theology and become a pastor. He was already a student at Chongshin Theological Seminary in Seoul. After completing his theological studies, he serves in three "Jesus Full Churches"(충만한 교회) in Mok-dong in Seoul, Ilsan, and Paju. These churches actively support missionaries in the world.

Hye-Soon Kim(김혜순) was one of those who studied the Bible with me. However, I did not help her well with Bible study. But she studied patiently. She became a good internal medicine doctor, opened the practice in Seoul, and treated many patients.

In my fourth year of university, I invited Myung-Hee Han(한명희) to our church. He had begun studying chemical engineering three years before me. He was then drafted into the military. After completing his military service, he returned to university. I invited him to study the Bible. He accepted my invitation and became a believer. He later married Young-Seo Kim(김영서), who had previously worked in Germany as a missionary and nurse. The couple later flew to Chicago, USA, as missionaries.

⋆ Grateful Seniors of the Church

I am also deeply grateful to the seniors who served the Lord in this student church.

First, I would like to thank Seon-Il Heo(허선일). He began studying chemical engineering at Chungnam University five or six years before me, served in the military for three years, and returned to the university in 1970. He was kind to all. He also gave me the booklet for daily Bible reading. Furthermore, he helped me and others discreetly in the background.

Medical student Hee-young Park(박희영) entered Chungnam University two years before me. I still remember his friendly and smiling face. When the reform movement of the UBF broke out in 1976, he suffered for some time from the loss feeling for his devotion to the church and left the church.

Yeol-Soo Eim(임열수) was a brilliant English student at Daejeon College. He often suffered from nosebleeds due to lack of sleep and hard work for his studies and the Lord's work. After graduating, he worked as an English teacher at a middle school in Daejeon. He married Seong-Ja Park(박성자) from our church and had a lovely daughter as their first child. When the UBF reform movement broke out in 1976, he suffered for a time from the feeling that he had lost much through his devotion to the church and left the church. Shin-Ok Kim(김신옥), pastor and chairman of his school's foundation, recognized his talent and faith and sent him with his wife to the United States to study theology. After receiving his doctorate, he returned and worked as the founding president of a "Gospel Theological College" in Daejeon and as pastor of a Gospel Church in Seoul. This case shows that God certainly blesses devotion to the Lord and His church.

Ki-Hyang Lee(이기향) was attending Daejeon Nursing School at the time of my studies. When my mother came to Daejeon to bring me rice and side dishes, she took my mother to our church and helped her believe in Jesus Christ. Thank you, Ki-Hyang Lee! After completing her studies, she flew to Germany as a nurse missionary. She then married Kang-Bok Lee of the Jongno Student Church in Seoul and worked with him, who was sent to Germany as leader of the student mission in Germany and dedicated himself to the mission in Germany.

⋆ My Friends in the Church

Young-Hwan Kim(김영환), a freshman and physics student at Daejeon College(now Hannam University), came to our church with classmates on a spring day in 1970 after the university sports festival. At that time, he was not a Christian. However, he came to faith through Bible study. After graduation, he worked for a time as a teacher at Yesan High School, my alma mater. He then transferred to a high school in Daejeon. From the first day he was faithful—faithful to the Lord, the church, his parents, and the school.

His wife, Bo-Young Lim(임보영), also served the Lord, the church, families, and those around them with unchanging faithfulness. The couple loves each other very much and has great respect for one another. Whenever I went to Daejeon Church, I was well served by this family with meals and acces to a bedroom. I was touched to see how much this couple respected each other and served their parents wholeheartedly. I was also moved to see that the couple's three children respected and loved their parents. I was also moved to see that the couple's three children respected and loved their parents.

⋆ **Beginning of the Daejeon CMI**

Here I briefly introduce the beginnings of our student church in Daejeon, where I came to believe in Jesus Christ. The original name of the student church in Daejeon was "Christian Student Center." After a few years it was changed to "University Bible Fellowship."

After the reform, the church name in Daejeon was changed to "All Nations Mission Church" in 2003 under the umbrella of the global church group "Campus Mission International."

Sarah Barry(born in 1930) and Melicent Huneycutt, missionaries from the USA, were sent to Korea by the Presbyterian Church in the USA in the mid-1950s.

Melicent Huneycutt-Vergeer(1926-2020; she married Mr. Vergeer when she was 60) founded the Christian Student Center in Daejeon in November 1962 with a group of seven freshmen from Daejeon College(now Hannam University). She had a Korean name, Mi-Seong Han(한미성), and was also active as a poet. She had friendly contact with the Korean poet Jeong-Ju Seo(서정주) and published his book of poetry, "Sillacho"(신라초), in English in 1962.

Jeong-Il Kim(김정일), one of the first seven members of the Daejeon CSC Church, served as pastor of the Myeongryun(명륜) CMI Church and as president of the International Theological Seminary.

Daejeon CSC started from the members of Daejeon College(now Hannam University). Bona Deok-Soon Hong(former pastor of Daejeon CMI), Soo-Min Lee(former professor of Hannam University), and Yeol-Soo Eim(former president of Gospel Theological University) are graduates of Daejeon College. In 1970 Young-Hwan Kim, Kwang-Bok Lee, Eun-Ok Kim, Hye-Min Seo, Young-Soo Woo, and many other freshmen from Daejeon College came to our church and studied the Bible.

Many from the Daejeon Nursing School also attended our church in 1970; for example, Shin-Young Yang(in her second year of the school, she immigrated to the USA), You-Kang Hur, Young-Suk Kim, and a year later, Bo-Young Lim, Young-Myo Shin, and Man-Woo Lee, etc. They learned the Bible, accepted Jesus, and gave themselves to the Lord.

Sixth Story: My Time as a Research Assistant at the University

"He told them, 'The harvest is plentiful, but the workers are few. Ask the Lord of the harvest, therefore, to send out workers into his harvest field.'" (Luke 10:2)

1. My Life as a Research Assistant

My Identity Card as a Research Assistant (March 1974 to February 1977)

In February 1974, I graduated from Chungnam University with honors, ranking second among all graduates, and received my bachelor's degree. In December 1973, I took the entrance exam for the master's program at the Seoul Academy of Sciences and failed. Later, I realized that God wanted me to stay in Daejeon for the time being so that I could later marry Esther and serve the Lord as a missionary in Germany. After failing the Academy of Sciences exam, I enrolled in the Graduate School of Chungnam University along with my classmates, Hwan-Young Kim(김환영) and Jun-Taek Shim(심준택), and worked as a research assistant in the Department of Chemical Engineering from March 1974 to February 1977. I earned 20,000 won a month(about $15 at the time). Our master's tuition fees were waived. Hwan-Young Kim chose Professor Ki-Seok Maeng(맹기석) as his master's thesis supervisor. He worked as a research assistant in the Department of Technical Education, while Jun-Taek Shim worked in the Department of Textile Engineering. After graduating from graduate school, Hwan-Young Kim worked as a senior researcher at the Korea Atomic Energy Research Institute in Daejeon. He was a gifted researcher and a kind person; I never saw him angry. Jun-Taek Shim was a good conversationalist and a capable businessman.

My master's thesis supervisor, Professor Bo-Sung Rhee(이보성), was a passionate researcher. During his work for his doctoral thesis at the University of Karlsruhe in Germany, he worked day and night in the laboratory. When I was in my second year, he taught us thermodynamics.

The first law of thermodynamics is called "the law of conservation of energy." Energy can be converted from one form to another, but it can neither be lost nor added. Simply put, "nothing can happen without something." Therefore, everything that exists - be it the universe or life–can come from nothing. For everything to exist, there must be a first cause. Thus, the world must have been "created" by a transcendent God. Only "God, the Creator" can overcome the first law of thermodynamics and create something out of nothing.

The second law of thermodynamics states that "all systems move in chaotic directions over time without external influences." This famous law is also known as the "law of entropy." Entropy here refers to the degree of disorder in a system. The greater the degree of disorder in the system, the higher the entropy. The law of entropy states that, without divine intervention, the entire universe is irreversibly moving toward disorder.

According to this law of thermodynamics, no orderly living being can arise without other living beings. From his teachings, I realized that Professor Rhee was searching for the truth. When I encouraged him to believe in God, he replied that he still had time to focus on research and would go to church after his retirement. A Catholic nun tried to lead him to faith in God. After his retirement, he became a Catholic.

My desk was on one side of the professor's room. The student chemistry laboratory was located in an extra building, about 40 meters from the lecture hall. One of my tasks was supervising the experiments of students, and another was the department's administrative work.

In my second year as a research assistant, Professor Bo-Sung Rhee created a small room for me to stay overnight by converting part of the laboratory hallway into a room. I have slept there since my second year of graduate school. There was also a shower room in the laboratory. I used an experimental heater in the lab to cook food for my meals.

In 1974, I, along with other research assistants, had a meeting with the university president, Hee-Beom Park(박희범). Previously, he had been an economics professor at Seoul National University and served as Vice Minister of Education under President Chung-Hee Park(박정희) in 1968 and then as Presidential Advisor on Economic Affairs. He was named as president of Chungnam University by President Chung-Hee Park in February 1973 and served until February 1977. I believe he led the hiring of the research assistants. He also made the decision to move Chungnam University from Munhwa-dong, Daejeon(대전시 문화동), to Yuseong, Daejeon(대전시 유성), with the help of the Korean government.

At these meetings with the research assistants, Hee-Beom Park said:

"Max Weber explained in his book <The Protestant Ethic and the Spirit of Capitalism> that Protestants caused the economic development of Western countries. Protestants who followed

Calvin's teachings worked hard to become rich but still lived thriftily. The money saved in this way became capital for economic development. The only exceptional nation that is not a Protestant nation and has nevertheless experienced an economic boom is Japan. Korea can also become a rich country if Koreans have hardworking and thrifty minds."

Through his story, I realized once again that God is the true source of all blessings.

In August 1976, I obtained the academic title of "Master of Engineering" with my diploma thesis "Carbonization of Oak Trees."

2. Life for the Happiness of Other People

In the spring of 1975, I shared a room in Daeheung-dong, near our church, with Jun-Chan Cho(조준찬), a pre-medical student, for several months. It was the only time I rented a room in Korea. After graduating from university, Cho became a doctor and opened his practice in Daegu. He served God faithfully as an elder in his church. His wife comes from a family that has been Christian for four generations.

While working as a research assistant in the Department of Chemical Engineering, I was able to continue serving our student church. Other male graduates, such as Nam-Sik Woo and Young-Hwan Kim, were required to serve for two and a half years in the military. The female graduates worked as teachers at schools or a bank employee: Jang-Won Son, Eun-Kyung Ahn, and Young-Gee Yoon as teachers and Seok-Hee Choi as a bank employee in Seoul.

In the evenings, I either attended the prayer meeting at church or led Bible studies with students. Il-Ju Lee and Young-Sook Kang had graduated from Gongju Nursing High School(공주 간호고등학교) and came from Gongju to receive missionary training. Missionary candidate Il-Ju Lee(이일주) studied the Bible with me for two months, and Young-Sook Kang(강영숙) studied with Jang-Won Son. They then received further missionary training at Jongno headquarters in Seoul and were sent to Germany as nurse missionaries.

Dong-Ju Lee(이동주), Il-Ju Lee's cousin, came to our church to meet Il-Ju Lee. He then studied the Bible with me, believed in Jesus, and dedicated himself to the Lord. He married Sook Kim(김숙), and the couple was sent to the United States as missionaries.

Around June 1976, UBF encountered a problem. Chang-Woo Lee(이창우, Samuel Lee) was the General Secretary of the UBF. Although he was not its founder, as general secretary he played an important role in the growth of the UBF in Korea and in sending missionaries to West Germany and the United States. After three gracious Bible conferences - the 1974 West German Summer Conference in Seewis, Switzerland; the 1975 West German Summer Conference in Frankfurt; and the 1975

USA Summer Conference near Niagara Falls - Chang-Woo Lee was probably a little more than proud of the work. He ordered excessive physical training for senior church leaders in Seoul. As a result, in June 1976, four senior church leaders of the UBF presented some reform points regarding Chang-Woo Lee's leadership in a circular. However, Chang-Woo Lee rejected their proposal, and a separation occurred. The four student churches that separated from UBF were located at Hanyang University, Yonsei University, Korea University, and Jeonju University. They named their group ESF(Evangelical Student Fellowship).

As a result of the reform movement, my senior graduate, Yeol-Soo Lim, and his wife, Seong-Ja Park, switched from our church to another church in 1976.

This incident showed me that mistakes can occur when the church is run not according to the teachings of the Bible, but according to human nature, regardless of whether a church has a distributed or centralized decision-making structure. One cannot simply say whether the centralized system of the Catholic Church is better or the decentralized system of the Protestant Church. Therefore, we must carefully examine God's will and follow the right path. This requires an open-mindedness, understanding of the opinions and feelings of others, and, above all, godly wisdom based on biblical truth.

This incident made me deeply aware that only God, no one else, is the true leader of our church. Even when people make wrong decisions and act wrongly, God carries out His will perfectly. Of course, this doesn't mean that God is responsible for people's lies or mistakes. People make mistakes and commit sins, but God doesn't make mistakes and doesn't sin. Yet God directs everything in the best way, so that everything works together for good. When we repent of our past mistakes, God forgives us. Therefore, we must admit our mistakes, accept God's forgiveness, and forgive others. This way, we can look positively toward the future.

The missionaries in West Germany were concerned about the problems in Korea. So, Chang-Woo Lee wanted to send Peter Suh(서 베드로) to West Germany to reassure the nurse missionaries. At the end of 1976, Peter Suh applied to the German Consulate for a three-month travel visa. During his trip to West Germany, he wanted to assign me to preach at the church in Daejeon and to help coworkers of the church.

At that time, I was working as a research assistant in the Department of Chemical Engineering. I explained the situation in our church to Professor Hong-Bin Lim(임홍빈), the dean of the department, and asked for his understanding that I would be working full-time for the church for about three months. The dean allowed me to do so. From December 1976 to the end of February 1977, I was able to serve the church full-time for three months, even though I was still a research assistant in the department.

Peter Suh assigned me to help student leaders through one-to-one Bible studies, and he helped the graduates. At that time there were about 20 student leaders in our church. I taught them the Bible personally, and those student leaders then taught the Bible to other students personally. Through this, I experienced God's love in abundance through God's Word and also through my Bible students, and I was overwhelmed with joy.

However, Peter Suh was unable to travel to West Germany because he was denied a visa. Since I very much enjoyed the full-time work of teaching the Bible to students, I resigned from my position as a research assistant at the university on March 1st. Peter Suh also sought a full-time assistant among the sisters, and Eun-Kyung Ahn volunteered. She left her job as an English teacher at the school and in December 1976 began working full-time at the student church.

And I visited not only Chungnam University but also Daejeon College, Daejeon Nursing School, and Mokwon College(목원 대학) to encourage student leaders. The students who personally studied the Bible with me were Su-Cheol Lee(이수철), his younger brother Su-Young Lee(이수영), Joo-Hoon Park(박주훈), and Sook-Hee Jeong(정숙희) from Daejeon College; Dong-Ju Lee (이동주, Joshua Lee in Seattle), Ki-Wook Koo(구기욱, Jeong-Won Koo's, 구정원, younger brother), Seong-Soo Han(한성수, Andrew Han in Canada), Myung-Ja Kim(김명자, Hannah Han in Canada), and Myung-Hee Hong(홍명희) from Chungnam University; Jeong-Hee Kim(김정희) from Mokwon College(목원대); Bok-Soon Lee(이복순, Esther Bae in Seattle), and Kyung-Soon You(유경순, currently the wife of John Oh, the pastor of Cheonan UBF) from Daejeon Nursing School.

Over time, most of them were scattered across the world, from Daejeon to many other nations, where they focused on spreading the Gospel and sharing the blessings of heaven through Bible study.

Seventh Story: Our Marriage and My Flight to Germany

"The man said, 'This is now bone of my bones and flesh of my flesh; she shall be called <woman,> for she was taken out of man.' That is why a man leaves his father and mother and is united to his wife, and they become one flesh." (Genesis 2:23-24)

"The third time he said to him, 'Simon son of John, do you love me?' Peter was hurt because Jesus asked him the third time, 'Do you love me?' He said, 'Lord, you know all things; you know that I love you.' Jesus said, 'Feed my sheep.'" (John 21:17)

1. Our Marriage

One day in early August 1977, I heard Peter Suh and Young-Hwan Kim discuss someone's marriage. I thought they were talking about the marriage of Young-Hwan Kim or someone else. I was having many one-to-one Bible studies with students at the time and received so much grace through them that I hardly thought about my marriage. But the two of them were talking about the marriage between Missionary Gil-Lye(Esther) Baek in West Germany and me.

Professor Bo-Sung Rhee, my master's course supervisor, had previously earned his doctorate at the University of Karlsruhe in Germany. I had therefore planned to pursue my doctorate in Germany; however, until then, no concrete way had been opened to me. But God opened this way for me at the right time through my marriage to Esther. Missionary Ki-Hyang Lee, who had been sent to West Germany from our church, wrote a letter to Peter Suh, the preacher of our student church, and proposed my marriage to Esther, who worked as a nurse's aide in Germany since 1970. She further wrote that after our marriage, I would come to West Germany as a missionary. Peter Suh first discussed this proposal with Young-Hwan Kim and then proposed marriage to me.

I immediately said yes and sent a letter to Esther asking her if she would like to marry me. I had exchanged letters with her several times since 1975 to encourage her missionary work. So, I already knew that she loved Jesus and did her best for the mission in Germany. I also knew that she was a middle school graduate. I wrote to her that I had answered Peter Suh with "yes" to the marriage proposal. Furthermore, I also told her that my right leg was injured and my hearing was a little impaired. And I asked her if she would marry me for the German mission. Meanwhile, Esther had been praying for a week since receiving the marriage proposal from missionary Hwa-Ja Lee. Then she sent me her letter and said, "Yes, with God's help."

After we decided to get married, we often exchanged letters. At that time, it took about a week for me to receive a letter from

Germany. During the day and evening I taught the Bible to the students one-to-one, and at midnight I wrote letters to her, about one letter every three days. I received her letters so many times. Our love was first love. After we decided to get married, our love was ignited so quickly through the exchange of letters. The letters we exchanged at the time were published as a book, "I Love You Fervently and Forever!" This collection of letters is a document of our declarations of love for each other and our declarations of love to the Lord Jesus Christ.

Together with Ki-Hyang Lee, Esther visited Professor Bo-Sung Rhee, who was researching in the Faculty of Chemical Engineering at the University of Dortmund. She introduced herself as my fiancée and explained that she needed an invitation from a doctoral supervisor in Germany for me. Professor Bo-Sung Rhee introduced me to Professor Schecker from the "Security Technology Research Group" as Esther's fiancée. And Professor Schecker promised her that he would write me an invitation letter as a doctoral student. At the time, South Korea did not issue passports to Koreans who wanted to study abroad on a self-financed basis to save foreign currency. In order to get an official invitation letter for me from Professor Schecker, Esther borrowed money from other Korean nurses and entrusted Professor Schecker with ten thousand marks. Professor Schecker then wrote an invitation letter, stating that he would pay my airfare and living expenses. As a result, I was able to get my passport and come to Germany with this invitation letter.

Esther arrived in Korea on October 7, 1977, to marry me. Peter Suh and I went to Gimpo Airport, which was the one and only international airport in Korea, and Pastor John Kim was there. I had received many letters from her, but I hadn't seen her yet. Out of curiosity, I looked at her passport photo, which was included in the book "The Light of People"(1974), a collection of testimonies from nurse-missionaries in West Germany. Her photo didn't look nice. When she came out of the airport exit, I was the first to recognize her and ran up to her. She was really beautiful and elegant, completely different from the photo in the book.

I came to the airport without flowers because I didn't know that I should give flowers when I greet someone at the airport. Pastor John Kim told me to get some flowers quickly and give them to Esther. So, I begged a strange lady for a single flower and gave it to Esther. It seemed to me that she was ashamed of the unattractive flower. We traveled together by highway bus from Seoul to Daejeon, where my home student church was located.

Our First Photo Together on October 7, 1977, and Our Wedding Photo

Esther, then, went to her hometown of Jangheung to visit her mother and family. She, then, returned to Daejeon and stayed at Peter Suh's apartment in Birae-ri(비래리). In those days, I was living in a hall of the church in Daeheung-dong. During the day, Esther studied the Bible with Peter Suh in the church, and I helped the students one to one with Bible study. In the evening, I ate with her at a restaurant, and escorted her to the apartment in Birae-ri, and returned to the church.

One evening we ate at a Japanese restaurant near Daejeon Central Station and walked towards the Birae-ri apartment. Not far from the apartment, we sat on a bench near the Seoul-Busan highway interchange. We stayed there so long that it was close to curfew at 24:00. After I sent Esther to the apartment, I had to sleep in a nearby inn.

Our wedding day was a Saturday in October 1977. Esther's

mother, brother, sister-in-law, elder sister, and relatives came to Daejeon from Jeonnam. On my side came my mother, my four sisters, my brother with his wife, the wife of my second maternal uncle, So-Hee Yeon(my grateful class teacher from the 6th grade), and In-Seop Lim(my former Bible student and the pastor of the Jesusfull-Church in Ilsan). Prof. Ki-Seok Maeng came as the representative of the professors in the Chemical Engineering Department. And Pastor John Jeon(General Secretary of UBF Korea), Samuel H. Lee(Preacher of UBF Hanyang in Seoul), Kang-Bok Lee(husband of missionary Ki-Hyang Lee), and Sook-Cheol Kim(former director of UBF in West Germany) came from Seoul. Nam-Sik Woo and Young-Hwan Kim, who had recently been discharged from the military, also attended the wedding.

Eun-Chun Lee(a hometown friend) and Deok-Ho Lee(이덕호, a friend from middle and high school, later a math professor at Gongju University) were also present. Peter Suh delivered the sermon, while Maria Yoo(유 마리아) sang a congratulatory song. Esther and I chose John 21:17 as our wedding verse because we were so grateful for Jesus' love for us and wanted to lead others and students to Jesus.

2. Esther's Testimony of Faith (presented early 1990s)

I. First, My Life without Jesus (1949-1974)

I was born i in Jeonnam Province in July 1948, the third and last child. My father was very calm and a so-called "Yangban"(

양반, which means "a man of noble class") with no income. My mother, on the other hand, was a very active and hardworking woman who did her best for her three children. But I liked my father much more than my mother. Although I had two siblings, my sister was 17 years older than me and my brother 14 years older than me, and I grew up like an only child. Still, my grandmother told me, I was very kind and obedient. When I was seven, my mother got very sick, and I had to take over her job. I cooked rice early in the morning and went to school afterward. Everyone felt sorry for me and praised me as a reasonable child.

The middle school was about 8 km from my house, which I almost always had to walk to. One day I was sent home from school during class because my parents couldn't pay school fees on time. I was shocked and very ashamed in front of my school friends. I wept a lot on the way home. Until then, my little world was still intact. I now complained to my mother that she had given birth to me despite her poverty. This incident left a deep wound in my heart. I became quiet so that I hardly talked anymore. My answer to each question was just a short "yes" or "no." Under the motto "Don't be rich, but never suffer from poverty" making money became my life's goal. Shortly after I graduated from middle school, my father fell ill. But we couldn't take him to the hospital because we didn't have money. I tried to help my father and family by working various jobs and learning crafts to earn money.

One day I decided to fly to Germany as a nurse aide to earn

money and started studying the nurse aide course in Korea. After graduation, I came to Germany in 1970. Until then, I firmly believed that I would be happy, if I earned money and helped my sick father and family members. Above all, I believed that my inner wound of humiliation would be healed. But that wasn't true. Life in Germany neither made me happy nor satisfied. Rather, I was lonely and sad in a foreign country. Today I know this: It wasn't life, but a desperate wandering in the darkness.

II. My Life with Jesus (since 1974)

In early 1973, Pastor Ok-Hi Park visited me. She had sent me the "Daily Bread Booklet" of the UBF by post and had prayed for my conversion since my arrival in Germany. Through her, the missionary Sarah K. Lee was introduced to me as my Bible teacher because she lived in Bochum, which is close to where I lived. With Sarah K. Lee, I learned the Word of God through the Book of Genesis. I was amazed at the Word of God from Gen 1:1 and 31:

"In the beginning, God created heaven and earth."

"And God saw all that He had made, and, behold, it was very good."

God created me for His joy. But I didn't live for God but for myself or for my family.

I was very happy because I discovered out the meaning of my existence in God Almighty.

Furthermore, based on Genesis 12:1-2, I took the first step in faith because God wanted to make me a blessing to others.

At the summer Bible conference in 1974 in Seewis, Switzerland, I met Jesus personally through the sermon by Shepherd Chang-Woo Lee, who preached it based on John 1:4, "In Him was life, and life was the light of people."

Until then, I could breathe in and out. But that wasn't true life. My life without Jesus was aimless and dark. That was because I was separated from God, and I lived for myself, which was a self-centered life, a godless life, and a money-centered life. And that was a sinful life of a sinner.

However, Jesus gave me the new life in Him and made my heart bright. So that I could experience the overwhelming joys of life - how joyful, how happy, and how completely free from all the pains of sadness and loneliness in a foreign land. When I accepted Jesus as Lord of my life and as my Savior, I was able to experience the grace of forgiveness. Because of His grace and love, I wanted to live my whole life for Jesus.

In 1977, under God's guidance, I founded a missionary family with Stephan to serve the student ministry by caring for the young souls on university campuses in Germany. Missionary Stephan Choe came to Germany on January 1, 1978, as the first student missionary from our church(University Bible Fellowship) so that I could find a specific mission for myself and pray for the German students at the universities. To serve this mission, I surrendered my Korean passport in 1983 and received a German ID card. My true home is neither Korea nor Germany, but the Kingdom of Heaven in Jesus Christ.

God, my gracious and patient Father, has blessed me to serve at the University of Dortmund for nine years, and He is now leading me to serve in a new ministry for students in Bochum. I don't speak German well and have never been a student, but God Almighty still wants me to take care of them as a faithful prayer servant to accomplish His work of redemption.

May God help me to serve the life-giving ministry well.

John 1:4: "There was life in Him, and this life was the light of men."

3. Honeymoon on Jeju Island

Nam-Sik Woo prepared the wedding and travel expenses at the church level, allowing us to spend the wedding and honeymoon without financial worries.

On the night of the wedding anniversary, we slept in the Yoo-Seong Soldier's Hotel(유성장병호텔) and attended the Sunday worship on the next day. After Sunday worship, we traveled by train to Busan for our honeymoon and then by ship to Jeju Island. Along the way, we made a short stop at the campus of Kyungpook University in Daegu and the campus of Pusan University in Busan. Then we took the car ferry from Busan to Jeju Island(제주도).

Arriving on Jeju Island(제주) at dawn, the first thing we did was find a motel room, read the Bible, and pray together. After that, we climbed Mount Halla(한라산). Mount Halla is 1,995 meters high. We took a bus to the middle of the mountain and hiked from there to the summit. Esther wore mountaineering clothes, while I wore a wedding suit. We had to climb a steep, rocky path near the summit. There were only low plants at the summit, and the volcanic lake "Baegnokdam"(백록담) had dried up. God gave us beautiful weather for our honeymoon, and from the summit of Mount Halla, we could see far away. I called out to Germany: "Germany is our bread!" That means, "We will give the Germans the bread of eternal life!" We were both filled with love, joy, and vision.

Left: On the Summit of Mount Halla on October 20, 1977
Right: At Cheonjiyeon Waterfall(천지연) in Seogwipo(서귀포) on October 21, 1977

The next day, after returning from Mount Halla, we took a bus to Seogwipo to see Cheonjiyeon Waterfall. At that time, Jeju Island was not very popular with tourists. Because of this, there were few tourists and the travel costs were cheap, so we could travel without any financial concerns.

After the trip to Jeju, we planned to visit Esther's parents' home to greet their family members in Jangheung. However,

Esther's brother wanted us to visit them later to have a party with the relatives. For this reason we did not visit Esther's home. I was very sorry that we didn't visit them.

On the way back from Jeju Island, we traveled to Shinryewon to visit my mother and family members. We got off the train at Shinryewon, took a taxi to my hometown for the first time in my life, and the taxi took us to the home where I was born.

Before I went to university, the house where I was born had three rooms. But at that time there was a fourth room right next to the gate. Esther and I stayed in the fourth room. There were no electric lamps, only oil lamps. It was too expensive to erect electricity pylons and connect power lines between a neighboring village and the house where I was born because my house was about 1 km away. So we had to light an oil lamp. Esther teased that I came from an ancient village. Her words were partly correct because I could have been a lumberjack of the Mountain Yonggol. Our God, however, was gracious to me in that He had freed me from poverty and curses and made me a person to share God's blessings with many people.

We returned to Daejeon on the Saturday of the honeymoon after staying in Shinryewon from Friday to Saturday. We had a week of honeymoon. Then we stayed the night in a room in Peter Suh's apartment in Birae-ri until Esther returned to Germany.

I registered our marriage at the city hall, listing our address as "488-17 Daeheung-dong, Jung-gu, Daejeon City(대전시 중구 대흥동 488-17)." At that time, in Korea, the date of submission of the marriage registration was marked as the date of marriage. So our marriage date on the document was October xx, 1977. And Esther returned to Germany on November 8.

4. My Passport Application

After Esther's flight back to Germany, I wanted to apply for a passport and visa so that I could fly to Germany as a student. Professor Bo-Sung Rhee recommended that I apply for a passport and visa through a travel agency, so I went to a travel agency in Seoul. However, a man at the travel agency said it was impossible to get a passport and an entry visa with an invitation letter from Germany. I decided not to seek any help from the negative-minded agency and to act on my own to obtain my passport and visa.

Jang-Won Son introduced me to her sister-in-law, Myung-Soo Kim(김명수), who worked in the Passport Department of the Foreign Ministry in Seoul. I went to the Passport Department and asked her for help. You can find out in detail how I got my passport with the help of Myung-Soo Kim in our letter collection, "I Love You Fervently and Forever!"

I thank Mrs. Myung-Soo Kim for her help; otherwise, it would have taken too long to get the passport. I flew to Germany on December 31, 1977, having received the travel authorization stamp from the Passport Department of the Ministry of Foreign Affairs on my passport in accordance with the treaty between the Korean and German governments.

Eighth Story: We Share the Good News with the Dortmund Students

"So God created mankind in his own image, in the image of God he created them; male and female he created them. God blessed them and said to them, 'Be fruitful and increase in number; fill the earth and subdue it. Rule over the fish in the sea and the birds in the sky and over every living creature that moves on the ground.'"
(Genesis 1:27-28)

"You are the light of the world. A town built on a hill cannot be hidden."
(Matthew 5:14)

1. Preparation for the Student Mission in Dortmund

* The Beginning of the German Mission by Korean Nurses and My Flight to Germany

Before I tell you about our student mission work in Dortmund, I would like to briefly mention the beginnings of mission work by our Korean nurses in Germany. The mission work of our church in Germany began on July 17, 1969, when the three nurse missionaries In-Kyung Seo, Dong-Ran Seol and Hwa-Ja Lee were sent from the student church in Daejeon to West Germany.

Subsequently, Sook-Cheol Kim from the church in Daejeon was sent to Germany on May 12, 1972, followed by Ki-Hyang Lee on June 29, 1972, also from Daejeon. Ki-Hyang Lee came to living faith through Bible study with Bona Hong of the Daejeon church and was sent to Germany as a missionary. From July 1972, she worked at the Bergmannsheil Hospital in Bochum for three years. She helped some nurses like Sun-Hee Lee(이선희), Kwan-Yeon(?관연), Jae-Gwan Yoo(유재관), and Mi-Ae Lee(이미애), who worked in Hagen and other cities, with the Bible study. Then Ki-Hyang Lee moved to Wuppertal in early 1976 and worked in a hospital there.

Mo	Tu	We	Th	Fr	Sa	Su
						1
2	3	4	5	6	7	8
9	10	11	12	13	14	15
16	17	18	19	20	21	22
23	24	25	26	27	28	29
30	31					

January 1978 and My Arrival at Frankfurt Airport on January 1, 1978

On the last day of 1977, at 1:24 p.m., I took the KAL flight from Gimpo Airport to Tokyo, Japan. I waited 8 hours at the Tokyo Airport and then transferred to the Japanese JAL flight. At that time, it was the Cold War era between democratic-liberal countries and communist countries, and planes from democratic-liberal countries were not allowed to fly over communist countries like China or the Soviet Union. My plane landed for refueling in Anchorage, Alaska, where it was covered in white snow. The plane landed at Frankfurt Airport at 8:34 a.m. on January 1. Until then, only Korean female missionaries from our Korean churches were active in West Germany. I was the first male missionary from our church in Korea to go to Germany.

Since there were hardly any trains at dawn on January 1, Esther, who lived in Rheda(Gütersloher Str. 64, 4840 Rheda-Wiedenbrück), had already taken the train to Frankfurt Airport on the evening of December 31, slept in the airport waiting room, and welcomed me. Ki-Hyang Lee and Sook-Hee Kim(김숙희) came to the airport from Wuppertal with the driver Sook-Hee Kim in a Volkswagen Beetle. Ki-Hyang Lee was on night duty and came to the airport sleepless.

When we arrived at the Mission Center in Wuppertal by car, Hwa-Ja Lee(이화자) came and greeted us warmly. After thanking God in prayer together, Esther and I took the train to Lippstadt to the hospital dormitory where Hwa-Soon Lee(이화순) worked. Lippstadt is located near Rheda-Wiedenbrück. Hwa-Soon Lee had reserved empty rooms in the Nurses' Dormitory so that we and others from Rheda could stay. The meeting was this year's Christmas party and took place on the first day of the New Year due to my arrival date. At that time, three missionaries worked in Rheda and Lippstadt. The two cities were the northernmost German cities where our missionaries worked. Therefore, these cities were named "the Northern District," and Hwa-Soon Lee was the district leader.

⋆ The First Prayer Meeting at the University of Dortmund

On the afternoon of Monday, January 2, 1978, Esther and I visited Prof. Dr. Schecker at the University of Dortmund, my doctoral supervisor. We also met Professor Hyuk-Jong Joo(주혁종), who had been my senior assistant in the Department of Chemical Engineering at Chungnam University. At that time, he was conducting research at the University of Dortmund. The three of us thanked God, who led us there for the Gospel work. I read Mark chapter 1, verse 1, and shared the message for the first time in my life in broken German, that God would bless this university and begin His work of evangelizing the students.Then we prayed to God together.

Esther and I were very grateful to God that we had finally reached the Holy Land promised by God, especially the University of Dortmund, and were allowed to begin preaching the Gospel there. Our gratitude to God at that time could be compared to the gratitude of Abraham, who left his homeland and reached the Promised Land of Canaan.

When Abraham was called by God to leave his homeland and arrived in Canaan, the Promised Land, he was so thankful to God that he built an altar there – a sign of his thanks.

In another review, our gratitude was comparable to the hearts of the Pilgrim Fathers in America. The Pilgrim Fathers, who had come to America from Europe on the ship Mayflower in 1620 in search of religious freedom, faced a harsh first winter. It was so cold that about half of them died from cold and disease within that year. But with grateful hearts they celebrated three days of

Thanksgiving in the fall of 1621 and thanked God profoundly. This was the beginning of the American Thanksgiving Day. Today, Thanksgiving remains a three-day holiday in the USA and is one of the most important holidays.

I was so grateful to God that He had saved me and Esther from the powers of death and hell, warmly welcomed us as prince and princess of the Kingdom of Heaven, and led us to Germany to share the heavenly blessings with Germans.

I was also overjoyed because I could serve God together with Esther.

⋆ The First Sunday Worship and the Bible Study Group in Rheda

Until then, the nurse missionaries in West Germany had not celebrated regular worship on Sundays because they lived in different cities and had to work every other Sunday. But for me, who had always held worship on Sundays in Daejeon, it was unthinkable not to hold worship on Sundays. So, our couple started celebrating the worship on Sunday, January 8, 1978. There were only two of us, and the place of worship was our room in the nurses' home in Rheda. Since Esther was on late duty that day, we celebrated worship at 9 o'clock in the evening. I preached in German with the title "The Beginning of the Gospel" from the Gospel of Mark 1:1-9. My German wasn't good, but Esther listened to my sermon as if it were an excellent sermon. And Esther presented her reflection on Romans chapter 1.

At this worship we thanked God that we had celebrated the

opening worship for pioneering the Uni Dortmund with Mr. Joo at the university on January 2 and were able to obtain another room in the nurses' home for my study on January 4.

From that Sunday on, we celebrated Sunday Worship in Rheda every week. Because I thought of Abraham, we were very grateful to God. Abraham had also worshiped God with his wife for many years, and God had graciously accepted his worship and blessed his family.

But when she saw that I hardly used the second room, she returned it a month later.

Earlier, when Sarah Ki-Hyang Lee had begun studying the Bible with Bona Hong in Daejeon, Korea, she fell ill and stayed in her dorm room. According to the rule, no males were allowed to enter the dormitory. However, Bona Hong had bravely entered the dormitory and taught Ki-Hyang Lee the Bible in her room. At that time, she had not yet made a firm decision to co-work in our church. However, after this Bible study, she decided to work together in our church. Because I remembered this story, I found it a little unusual for me to live in a nurses' dormitory, and I was grateful for that.

On some weekdays, Bible studies were held under Esther's leadership with several nurses. Some of Esther's colleagues participated in these Bible studies, such as Marion, Ellinor, Purin, Gaby, Wilfriede, Dong-Ok Kim(김동옥), Hie-Za Kim(김희자), etc. Doo-Kyoo Kim(김두규), Dong-Ok's husband, came to study the Bible depending on his situation. Ellinor was a nurse, about 35 years old at the time. Purin was a Filipino woman, around 25 years old. Dong-Ok Kim and Hie-Za Kim were Korean.

In addition to this group Bible study, Esther taught Purin the Gospel of Mark and Hie-Za Kim Genesis and Romans through individual Bible study. I thank God that He used Esther as a faithful Bible teacher and prayer warrior for them. She is a very precious daughter of God.

I began to pray for the people at the University of Dortmund, e.g., Glenz Horst(assistant in the Chemical Engineering Department), Pilger Bernd(technician), Keller Gert(technician in the Technical Chemistry Department B), Hyuk-Jong Joo, etc.

⋆ My Attendance at the German Courses at the University of Münster and the University of Bochum

From Monday, February 13, 1978, I attended the German course at the University of Münster every day. I got up at 5:30 in the morning and took the slow train from Rheda to Münster.

Once, in February 1978, Prof. Hans-Georg Schecker came to Münster to apply for a room in the dormitory for me. He did so much for me. May God bless him, his family, and his descendants.

However, I commuted from Rheda to Münster because I thought that praying with Esther was much more important than saving time by living in Münster.

The participants in the German course in Münster were truly international. During the break in class, I heard the sounds of different languages from all over the world: Turkish, Persian,

African French, etc. Everyone spoke their own language or broken German. It was just loud.

On Thursday, February 16, I spoke to a German student in Münster. His name is "Heinz"; he was studying medicine in his first semester. I was happy as if I had won the whole world, even though I hadn't talked to him about Bible study. But it is true that a person is more valuable than the whole world. On March 5, I met another German student named Alfred Krusenbaum and prayed for him.

Among the German course participants was a Korean student named Jung-Ran Yoo(유정란). She told me that the German course at the University of Bochum was much better than the one in Münster. I then informed Mr. Schmidt of my wish at the International Office of the University of Dortmund. He informed me that I could attend the German course at the University of Bochum starting in April. At that time, Germany was still economically prosperous. The German course at the University of Bochum was scheduled to begin in April. Esther tried to find a new job in a hospital in Dortmund to be able to work there from April 1978. But at first, she couldn't find a job. That's why she accepted a job offer from the Evangelical Nursing Home in Schwerte. Schwerte is a southern suburb of Dortmund. She was scheduled to start work there on April 1, 1978. Marion, a colleague of Esther's in Rheda, took us to Schwerte in her VW Polo. We could move to Schwerte with all our belongings in the little car. We had so little for the move from Saxony because we had no furniture, and Esther had previously lived in the nurses' dormitory. In Schwerte, we lived again in a room of the nurses' dormitory(Ostberger Str. 34, 5840 Schwerte/Ruhr). Esther walked to work, about 100 meters to the nursing home. She became pregnant there around mid-May.

I must tell the story of my encounter with Soon-Ki Yoon(윤순기) here. I was in Bochum at the end of March or April 1 to look for a room for the German course at the University of Bochum. I met Soon-Ki Yoon there, who had graduated from Jungang University(중앙 대학교) in Seoul. He had recently come from Korea and was temporarily staying in his friend Jun-Young Kim's room(김준영) in the student dormitory "Auf der Papenburg," which is very close to our current apartment.

I stayed in this room with him one night, and the next day I went with him to look for an apartment. At the time, I had no idea how to find a room. Our search for a room that day was unsuccessful. I drove back to Schwerte and realized that God wanted me to stay with Esther and pray to God together before we started the student mission. I lived in the nurses' home in Schwerte, and from the beginning of April, I commuted daily from Schwerte via Dortmund to Bochum for a German course.

One day in the spring, I received a notification from the Office of Student Affairs at the University of Dortmund that I could move into room No. 142 of the student residence at Ostenbergstraße 99 in Dortmund on June 1 of the same year, because Prof. Schecker had requested a room for me.

I went to the dormitory and found that it was too far from the university, so I returned the offer and continued to live with Esther in Schwerte. The dormitory is actually not far from the university; you can walk from the dormitory to the university in five minutes. At the time, however, I thought it was too far because I believed that a dormitory should be at the university, like the dormitories in Korea.

Given the great(?) distance, I thought of God's will and came to the conclusion that God wanted me to stay with Esther and to prepare for the salvation of the students through our common prayer. So God helped me to stay with Esther in Schwerte and to pray with her.

The German courses included elementary and intermediate levels, and one level lasted one semester. I started with the basic level, and Dr. Stratmann, the director of the German course, taught our elementary course. After about a month, she proposed I move to the intermediate course. Ms. Hälmemann(?) and Ms. Kunau taught this course. I really enjoyed the German course.

⋆ The Reason Why Esther and I Changed Our Names

Most Koreans write their family name "최" as "Choi." However, I wrote "Choe" as a family name on my passport application so that Germans could pronounce my family name correctly. My attempt, however, was only half successful. I thought of the English consonant "ch" and wrote Choe. But if you want to pronounce the Korean consonant "ㅊ" correctly in German, you have to write "tsch." Because "ch" is pronounced similarly to "k" in German, "Choe" is pronounced similarly to "Koe." This led to Germans who met me for the first time mispronouncing our family name. My Korean first name was Myeong-Hwan(명환). I liked my Korean first name.

When I was sent out to Germany, Peter Suh had proposed that I use my first name, "Stephan," in Germany. He had suggested this name because I had once preached a sermon about the faith of Stephan from the Book of Acts. But I was afraid of dying a martyr, so I didn't like his suggestion at first. Thus, I continued to introduce myself as Myeong-Hwan Choe.

When I started taking the German course in Bochum, I met some German students and introduced myself to them as "Myeong-Hwan"(명환). But they couldn't pronounce my name correctly or remember it. My first name was too difficult for them to recall. When I introduced myself as "Stephan," they could immediately respond, "Hello, Stephan!" I understood why European missionaries adopted Korean names while serving in Korea. The German diplomat who played an important role in the opening of Korea and for the Korean mission was Paul Georg von Möllendorff. For the Koreans, he posed as In-Deok Mok(목인덕). Since then I have used "Stephan" as my first name. After understanding the significance of the name change for the German Mission, I suggested that Peter Suh could also give my wife a new name. That's how she became Esther.

When our first son was born, we named him "Siseong"(지성). Esther and Siseong initially received German citizenship because I had to wait a little longer for my doctorate. When

I received German citizenship, I changed my first name to "Stephan Myeong-Hwan" to distinguish it from the name of our first son, which was changed to Stephan. Since Germans often don't use middle names, my first son and I get confused from time to time. For example, the election commission's two invitation letters for my son and me said "Stephan Choe" and "Stephan Choe."

2. The Years of the First House Church at "Ostenbergstraße 22" in Dortmund (August 15, 1978 – September 28, 1981)

⋆ Our Move to Ostenbergstraße 22

On August 15, 1978, we moved from the nurses' residence in Schwerte to an apartment at Ostenbergstraße 22 in Dortmund. It was a Tuesday and a Catholic holiday, "Assumption of Mary." Since we had lived in a nurses' residence until then, we didn't have to move much. Our new apartment belonged to the Karius family, the owners of "Flowers of Karius." This family ran a flower shop with a greenhouse. Our apartment was on the second floor of the house and had two connecting rooms, a small shower room with a toilet, and a very small kitchen.

The entrance door to the apartment was located between the kitchen and the shower room. The apartment was about 40 m^2. This Bible house was like a manger in which Jesus lay after His birth. We were very grateful to God for this Bible House. Stephan, our first son, was born while we were living in this apartment. Students like Martin Nachtrodt and Ludger

Sickelmann came to study the Bible and taught others the Bible.

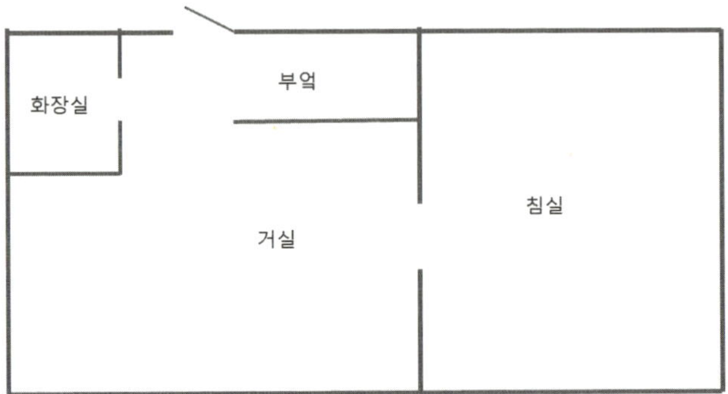

House Church at Ostenbergstraße 22 in Dortmund: August 15, 1978 – September 28, 1981

On the second floor on the right-hand side was our house church.

At the time, I had no information about the German ticket system. I wanted to drive from Dortmund-Barop via Dortmund Central Station to the German course at the University of

Bochum. Back then, you only needed a single ticket for the tram within a city. Because I had to change trams once to get from Dortmund-Barop to Dortmund Central Station, I bought two tickets. Sometime later, I found out that I had bought two tickets unnecessarily. Above all, neither I nor Esther had known that there were inexpensive monthly tickets, so I had bought tickets every day. Although Esther had lived in Germany since 1970, she had only occasionally traveled with a one-time ticket.

*** Cooperation with Missionaries in Essen for the Essen-Bochum-Dortmund Student Mission**

From May 15, 1978, following a reorientation by Abraham Lee and You-Kang Hur(허유강, married Cho/조), we began working with the missionaries in Essen. We wanted to concentrate our missionary work on a few major cities such as Dortmund-Bochum-Essen, Wuppertal-Cologne, Frankfurt, and Stuttgart. After a year, several strategic mission districts were established in Dortmund, Cologne, Frankfurt, and Stuttgart. Based on this new mission strategy, Esther and I began working with You-Kang Hur, Sara Oh, and Bok-Eum Lee(이복음) in Essen. You-Kang Hur was a Korean nurse missionary. She had begun her nursing studies in Daejeon, South Korea, at the same time as I did in 1970. She had come to believe in the Bible at our Daejeon student church. During her studies, she had served as student leader of the mission group at her nursing school.

After completing her three-year study, she came to Germany on January 8, 1974, as a nurse missionary. At that time, many

Korean nurses were coming to West Germany to earn money. She, however, had come to Germany for missionary purposes. Her heart burned for the salvation of souls. She worked the night shift to invite young people to Bible studies during the day. Ebraim Analonyi, a Persian student at the University of Essen, attended the 1978 Seewis Summer Conference at her invitation. She also led a student, Eli(Ellenore Beter), to the Bible conference. The summer conference was held from September 19 to 22, 1978, in Seewis, Switzerland.

You-Kang invited many other students, including Regine and Gabrielle, to Bible studies, Sunday worship at the church and Bible conferences. You-Kang prayed for a long time for Barbara Hebenstreit, a student at the University of Essen.

Soon-Ki Yoon, who was taking a German course with me, worked with us. He also participated in the summer Bible conference in Seewis.

In the second half of 1978, we were very actively involved in the student missions in Dortmund, Bochum, and Essen. Sara Houngum Oh(오현금, Sara Chang) had come to Germany as a nurse's aide after graduating from high school. She had come to faith in 1975 through the Bible study with Yang-Nim Hwang(황양님). In 1978, she worked in Essen-Kupferdreh. She prayed for her friends, such as Ae-Sik(애식) and Young-Hee(영희) Kornowski in Essen, among others. Y.-H. Kornowski was a wise woman and had a talent for Korean dance. Therefore, she began studying dance at the Folkwang Musikhochschule in Essen. After marrying Peter Kornowski, she stopped her studies to take care of her family. However, she continued to develop her talent in her free time. Her husband understood her well. Together, they were committed to promoting Korean culture. Mrs. Kornowski heads the Asian Culture Association in Essen, which is dedicated to promoting Korean and Asian culture.

Foreign students were required to take the German Language Examination(PNdS) before beginning their studies. This exam consisted of grammar, dictation, text rendering, and oral exams. I passed the exan without any difficulties in October 1978. After this exam, I attended lectures in the Chemical Engineering Department at the University of Dortmund. However, I couldn't understand the professor's lecture and had headaches. I wondered whether it would have been better for me to attend the German course for a longer time.

⋆ My Mother Went to Heaven

In February 1979, we were expecting the birth of our first child. Esther had to take the train to Schwerte to work there. Abraham Lee visited us once and suggested sending the child to my mother in Korea to babysit after the birth. In fact, some missionaries sent their first children to their parents in Korea for babysitting. But I was appalled by his proposal and rejected it immediately. I was convinced that Esther and I should raise our children ourselves. I asked my mother in Korea if she could come to Germany to babysit. She agreed, even though she was supposed to be babysitting my brother's young children in Korea. And Esther and I were expecting my mother.

However, in early February, my brother called me and told me that my mother had passed away from a stroke on January 19, 1979. According to the lunar calendar, her date of death is December 21, 1978, which commemorates her death anniversary according to the lunar calendar. My brother did not notify me of her death immediately, so I had to take an expensive flight to Korea.

In early January 2000, Dr. Renate Schmeinck and I flew to Korea with Samuel Cheon-Gi Park(박 사무엘 천기) and took him to the hospital because he was ill. I stayed in Korea for about a month.

While visiting my fourth sister in Daeryul, Yesan(예산 대률), I drove with her on January 7 to my parents' grave in Dongmak, Shinryewon-ri, Yesan(예산 신례원리 동막), near our birthplace. My mother, a young widow due to the early death of our father, had worked hard in the fields to raise six children.

Of course, I regret that my mother died early. However, I thank God that within a few days, He allowed my mother, who worked hard in the fields to raise her children, to fall asleep peacefully, allowing her to enter the Kingdom of Heaven without pain and enjoy the bliss of eternal life. Our God is gracious.

After visiting my parents' grave, we drove to our childhood home in Teojinmok(터진목). An old woman lived there with her son. I grew up in that house until I graduated from high school.

⋆ Sara Oh Moves to Dortmund, and You-Kang Cho Flies to Korea

Starting in June 1978, we actively invited students from Essen, Bochum, and Dortmund to Bible studies and Sunday worship in the church. You-Kang Cho came to Dortmund after her night shift, prayed with us for the students, and then returned to Essen to sleep.

The invited students showed interest in Bible studies. Over time, however, we realized that it was more effective to initially focus our work on the students in one city, as inviting students from other cities to Dortmund for worship was too time-consuming for them. Sara Oh(Chang), who had previously worked in Essen, moved to Dortmund on December 29, 1978; she found a new job at Mary's Hospital in Dortmund-Hombruch. And You-Kang Cho flew to Korea on April 4, 1979, to work with her husband, Seong-Ki Cho(조성기), in the student ministry at Seoul National University.

After Sara Oh moved to Dortmund, she actively helped many students with the Word of God. At her invitation, Adi Satria came to the Sunday worship for the first time on January 21, 1979, learned the Bible, and worked with us. Sara also helped Ae-Sik Kim(김애식, her friend), Sook-Bin Lee(이숙빈, a student at the Folkwang College of Music in Essen), Detlef Hauerkampf in Dortmund, and Y.H. Kornowski(her friend in Essen) with their Bible study. Sook-Bin Lee began studying the Bible in the spring of 1979 and attended the summer conference. Detlef Hauerkampf began studying the Gospel of John on June 23, 1979. Sara also helped Martina, Hee-Sook(희숙), Gaby, Theo, and others.

When Martin R. moved out of his apartment next to ours after graduating in 1980, Sara Oh moved there. So she lived on the second floor next to our apartment. She looked after little Stephan from time to time while Esther slept after her night duty. One day, she looked after Stephan in her apartment while Esther slept. While she was briefly busy doing something, little Stephan climbed onto the windowsill and fell outside. Thank God he wasn't hurt because there was nothing dangerous on the ground.

Prof. Schecker, my doctoral supervisor, had a working group on "Physical-Chemical Process Engineering and Safety Engineering" at the Chemical Engineering Department at the University of Dortmund. He put a table and a chair for me in a room at the university so I could study there.

To get my Korean diploma recognized, I was supposed to take three recognition exams: thermodynamics, thermal process engineering, and technical chemistry. For a year I studied for these recognition exams and passed them.

⋆ Birth of Our First Son, Babysitting, and the Steinecke Family

In mid-February 1979, Esther suspected that she was about to give birth because she noticed that labor was starting about a week before the due date. So, she packed her things that day and drove to the Dortmund City Clinic. After the exam, the doctor told her to go home and come back when she was in real labor. However, Esther asked to stay in the hospital because she thought she would soon give birth to a baby. It was a Tuesday.

Sara Oh and I had a Bible study that evening around 7 p.m. After the Bible study, Sara went out and called the hospital from the phone booth. At that time, we didn't have a phone at home. She then learned that Esther had already given birth to a baby. So, she and I drove to the hospital.

At that time, maternity leave was about a month after giving birth. We didn't have a babysitter. It was very inconvenient for her to go to work in Schwerte a month after the birth. For this reason, that's why Esther went out of work for about a few months.

I went to the social welfare office in Dortmund-Hombruch to inquire about the possibility of receiving social assistance. We were then contacted by a social worker. The social worker helped me find a scholarship opportunity. To receive the scholarship, I needed two recommenders. Prof. Schulz wrote me a recommendation letter because I had passed the oral thermodynamics test for the recognition of my diploma in Korea. Prof. Schecker wrote another recommendation based on my work as a research assistant for him. As a result, I received 800 marks per month in the first year and 500 marks in the second year, because Esther worked that year.

After a few months of unemployment, Esther found a new job at the Evangelical Hospital Bethanien in Dortmund-Hörde. Esther worked the night shift because we didn't have a babysitter. She wanted to take care of the baby herself during the day whenever possible. We had a small apartment with a living room and a bedroom. However, there was no door in the passage between the two rooms. Esther tried to sleep while baby Stephan lay next to her. However, because of the baby, she couldn't sleep properly and had to wake up often. For that reason, I didn't go to university but took care of our baby in the living room so that Esther could sleep well in the other room.

When I was single, I didn't like kids because they bothered me. But I thought it was more important to take care of my child than to prepare for my doctorate. I tried to let the baby play as quietly as possible in our living room. But it wasn't easy. Esther often woke up to the sounds of the baby playing. When the baby began to walk, she found it much harder to sleep. I even took the baby to the university laboratory a few times. Prof. Schecker and assistants liked Stephan and had a good understanding of my situation. I thank God and them for that. I am also very grateful to God for this too, because I didn't feel like I was wasting time because of the babysitting. Rather, I enjoyed taking care of our child because I knew that caring for the child was much more important than my doctoral thesis.

The attic apartment of the Steinecke family (Ostenbergstr. 21)

One day in the early fall of 1980, I didn't go to the university because of Stephan's babysitting and walked up and down Ostenbergstraße with little Stephan while Esther slept after the night duty. Ilse Steinecke, a neighbor who lived at Ostenbergstraße 21, saw this. She offered to look after Stephan for free. She was like an angel to us. Her husband, Dr. Volkmar Steinecke, worked at Hoesch Company in Dortmund-Hörde. He also gave statistics lessons at the University of Clausthal. Mrs. Steinecke already had Jan as a foster child. After Stephan, she also looked after our missionaries' children free of charge, such as Rebecca Han's daughter Maria, Sara Chang's daughter Mira, and our second son, Timothée. Her daughter Helga also helped the small children with her mother. Mrs. Steinecke brought our children home-baked birthday cakes on every birthday until they turned 18 years old. She still contacts Maria, who is now working as a doctor in Berlin.

The Steineckes loved Northern European countries like Iceland and Scandinavia, enjoyed traveling to these countries, and promoted cultural exchange between the city of Dortmund and Scandinavian countries. Until his death in 1995, he served as the first chairman of the German-Icelandic Society.

He held a high position at Hoesch Company. However, his family lived in an attic apartment with three small rooms without a television and with a relatively large garden. This family led a generous, helpful life. The Steineckes had an open, compassionate nature. They were humble, friendly, and cheerful.

When I was on my way to the Bible conference in December 1983, Esther stayed home because she was heavily pregnant for the second time. She drove to the hospital a little earlier than expected. Mr. Steinecke took her to the St. Johannes Hospital in Dortmund for delivery in his car. The doorman mistook him for a taxi driver.

In 1995, Mr. Steinecke was diagnosed with cancer. Chemotherapy didn't help him. Shortly before his death, his wife called me and asked me to provide him with pastoral care. I went to him. There were two of us in the room, him and me. I told him about Jesus' death for our sins and His resurrection for us and asked him if he personally believed in it. He nodded. Although he didn't share a specific story, he expressed feelings of regret. After a day or two, I heard that he had seen heaven open and angels. Shortly afterward, he fell asleep. I thank God for giving him peace and leading him into the Kingdom of Heaven.

After he passed away, many people from Germany and Scandinavian countries gathered for the memorial service at the Waldorf School in Dortmund-Stockum. Many recounted how kind and compassionate he was and how much good he did for others.

3. The Years of the Second House Church at "Baroper Bahnhofstraße 73" in Dortmund (September 29, 1981 – May 31, 1984)

⋆ Reason for the Move of Our House Church

We had been living at Ostenbergstraße 22 in Dortmund since August 15, 1978. In the meantime, new missionaries from Korea had arrived. Some German coworkers also worked with us. Since the apartment was too small for the Sunday worship, we wanted to move to a larger apartment to have enough space. Then we saw an advertisement in the newspaper 'Ruhr Nachrichten':

Barop, Bahnhofstraße, comfortable apartment, 4 rooms, kitchen, bathrooms, loggia, 145 sqm, underfloor heating, separate entrance, also suitable as an office or practice, rent by arrangement. Tel: Do 71 80 20

On Saturday, September 26, 1981, we moved into this larger

apartment at Baroper Bahnhofstraße 73, opposite the Barop Railway Station.

The Second House Church at the Baroper Bahnhofstraße 73 in Dortmund (First Floor of the House). September 28, 1981 – May 31, 1984

Our house church was on the first floor. It was opposite the old Barop Train Station, which at that time served as a fruit market called "Fruit Market." The house church had four rooms: a large living room and three smaller rooms. Rebecca Han lived in the entrance room (to the right of the entrance door). After Rebecca moved out, Karl-Heinz Hohmann moved in and lived there for about one year.

The Danko family lived on the second floor of the building. This couple was very kind to us and occasionally looked after Stephan.

I stayed in the City Clinics from September 28 to October 8, 1981, for chronic otitis media and had ear surgery.

At some point, the bedbugs appeared in our bedroom. We didn't know whether they came from old mattresses or from the apartment. At night, they climbed the walls, fell from the roof above us, and bit us. So we called the health department of the city so that an employee of the health department came and sprayed bedbug repellent. As a result, the bugs disappeared from the apartment.

⋆ On Our Wedding Day, I Failed My First Driver's License Test

In March 1983, Esther became pregnant for the second time. In September of that year, Stephan was diagnosed with hepatitis. He had to stay alone in an isolation room at the Dortmund-Benninghofen Municipal Children's Hospital for six weeks in September and October. I cycled there every day and played games like Lego with him. Esther, with her heavy body, had to take the bus because of her pregnancy.

That spring, my mother church in Daejeon, Korea, had sent 1,000 marks so we could buy a French car, the Dyane-6, for church work. Of us, however, only Rebecca Han had a driver's license from Korea. She had only practiced driving in the practice area and couldn't drive well on the city streets. Ludger Sickelmann didn't have a driver's license, but he grew up in the country and was good at driving. One evening, Rebecca Han, Ludger, and I drove the Dyane-6 to the empty parking lot of the University of Dortmund to practice driving. When we got there, I would have liked to practice driving first. But I thought, as a preacher, I should yield to Rebecca and let her practice driving first. When she had driven a bit with the help of Ludger, the police came and asked her to show them her driver's license.

Rebecca said she left her driver's license at home. The police told her to drive home and show them her driver's license. Rebecca drove the car at duck speed, and Ludger helped her from the passenger seat. On the way on Ostenbergstraße near the dormitory, the police stopped us because Rebecca was driving too slowly and suggested that Ludger drive our car instead of her. Ludger replied that he did not have a driver's license. When Ludger suggested to the police that one of the police officers could drive our car, they replied that they were not allowed to do so. So, Rebecca had to continue to drive slowly to the house and show them her international driver's license. The police told her, "Drive carefully!" and drove away. From this incident, I have learned that the way to life is to follow the teachings of the Bible and "to yield to others."

I attended the Szymanski Driving School in Dortmund and practiced driving for more than 50 hours. My driving test day was one day in October. First there was the theoretical(written) test at the driving school, which I passed without any problems. This was followed by the practical driving test on the road. I sat in the driver's seat, the driving instructor sat in the passenger seat to my right, and the examiner sat in the back. I drove for about 30 minutes without difficulty and stopped at an intersection because the traffic light was red. I thought that if I just crossed that intersection, I would get my driver's license. When the traffic light turned green, a truck in the left lane turned left, and a car in front of me crossed the intersection. I forgot that the rear of the left-turning truck would be slightly over the right lane and wanted to cross the intersection, but the driving instructor braked our car hard to avoid a collision with the truck. The instructor reprimanded me harshly. Needless to say, I failed the test.

When I got home and told Esther about it, she was very sad. She had hoped that we could visit Stephan by car from that day forward. Above all, the day was our wedding anniversary. And I still had to visit Stephan by bike, while Esther, with her big belly, took the bus.

⋆ Timothée's Birth

In mid-December 1983, a Bible conference took place in Rehe over the weekend. On Friday afternoon, I drove with others to the conference in Rehe in the Westerwald. Esther stayed home because Timothée, our second son, was about to be born. Her due date was around Christmas, but Esther realized she could give birth a little earlier. When she noticed contractions, she asked Mr. Volkmar Steinecke, the husband of the babysitter Ilse, to take her to the St. Johannes Hospital in Dortmund. There, Esther gave birth to Timothée quickly and without complications, just as she had with our first son, Stephan.

When I returned from the Bible conference on Sunday, the baby was already lying next to her. I thanked God for taking care of her and the baby. Esther was happy that she had, as she had hoped, a boy. Stephan was also happy about the birth of his brother. Timothée has a fine sense of feeling and intelligence. His character is more like his mother's. Stephan is loyal and determined. His character is similar to mine. Stephan liked to take his brother to his school and was proud of him. Timothée preferred playing with his brother to going to kindergarten.

4. The Years of the Third House Church at 'Helenenbergweg 7' in Dortmund (June 1, 1984 – February 28, 1987. From July 31, 1986, used only as a church)

⋆ New House Church

The Third House Church in Dortmund, Helenenbergweg 7 (first floor). and Esther with Timothée

June 1, 1984 – February 28, 1987
(From July 31, 1986 onwards, it was used only as a church.)

Because Walter and Ludger, important co-workers in Dortmund, had moved to Cologne and the number of students attending church services had decreased slightly, we changed our Bible house. The Third House Church in Dortmund was a 2-room apartment of about 60 m^2 and was about 50 m from the tram stop 'An der Palmweide,' making the apartment quiet yet easily accessible by tram. The apartment was heated by an electric floor heating system, so we felt like we were in an apartment in Korea with a floor heating system. Although the heating costs were relatively expensive, we were happy to sleep on the floor. There was some empty space and allotments across the street. There was a lot of snow that year, so Stephan could go sledding there with Timothée.

Stephan attended the Ostenberg Elementary School right next to an old church called the 'Margarethenkapelle' in 'Klein Barop' near our apartment.

One day at noon, Stephan came home from school with a broken umbrella. He said that some boys had broken the umbrella. So, Esther was very concerned for Stephan's safety. Several years passed. In the meantime, we had moved to Bochum. And Stephan visited Korea during the summer vacation and did the Bible study at Hanyang UBF with Lydia Lee, who was in Korea at the time. After Stephan came back from Korea, he asked Esther for forgiveness because he had broken the umbrella himself for fun and lied to Mama. Of course, we were pleased with his repentance and honesty.

Our attic apartment at the Baroperstrasse 204.
We lived on the right side of the street from August 1, 1986 to February 28, 1987.

On August 1, 1986, our family moved to Baroperstrasse 204 to separate the church from our home. Our home was an attic apartment with electric night storage heating.

One weekend, from Friday to Sunday, there was a Bible conference. Because children preferred to stay at home, we asked our landlady, who lived on the first floor of the same house, to take care of our children. After the Bible conference, we came back by car. When Timothée saw us at the entrance to the house, he was very happy. While I was getting our things out of the trunk and then pressing the car tailgate down to close the trunk, Timothée sprinted towards me at lightning speed, causing the car tailgate to hit his head. Blood flowed from his head. We were shocked and drove straight to the doctor for an examination at the hospital. We could only calm down after it was found that his injury was minor.

After we moved to Bochum on February 28, 1978, the Dortmund church relocated to the apartment on the first floor of the Hanibal skyscraper at Vogelpothsweg 18, which was located about 800 meters northeast of the university.

*** My PhD**

The topic of my thesis was the flash point of flammable liquid mixtures. The flash point is the lowest temperature at which sufficient flammable gases form above the liquid to allow combustion by an ignition source. For example, lighting a cigarette with a match in a room containing volatile and flammable liquids can cause a fire or explosion. The flash points of many pure flammable liquids were already known at that time. However, the flash points of liquid mixtures were largely unknown. I measured the flash points of several liquid mixtures experimentally. I also calculated the flash points of the flammable liquid mixtures in advance.

I completed my doctoral thesis around 1985. However, my German wasn't good. Professor Schecker began correcting my thesis. He corrected some parts; however, the correction was time-consuming. Therefore, Professor Schecker assigned an assistant to correct it. The assistant corrected my dissertation when he found time. The correction took about a year. I am very grateful to Professor Schecker and the assistant for their help.

Prof. Schecker published some of the results of my doctoral thesis twice in specialist journals[3]. The list of some theses

---

3) **Choe M.-H., Gmehling J., Schecker H.-G.** : *Flammpunkte von binären brennbaren Flüssigkeitssystemen mit Mischungslücke.* Chem.-Ing.-Techn. 56(1984), 44 - 46

Choe M.-H., Schecker H.-G. : *Flammpunkte von polynären* supervised by Prof. Schecker can be found on the University of Dortmund website[4].

Kalkert, N.;
Rindfleisch, H.-N.: *Untersuchung zur Methodik von Sicherheitsanalysen*; Universität Dortmund; 1984

Alfert, F.: *Sicherheitstechnische Kenngrößen von polynären Brennstoff/Luft-Gemischen [Brennstoff-Luft-Gemischen] und selbstzerfallenden Stoffen*; Universität Dortmund; 1985

Choe, M.: *Experimentelle und theoretische Untersuchungen zur Flammpunktbestimmmung von Flüssigkeitsgemischen*; Universität Dortmund; 1986

Mähler, R.: *Zur Prozeßführung bei der Herstellung von Elastomer-Metall-Verbundelementen*; Universität Dortmund; 1991

At the end of 1985, Prof. Bo-Sung Rhee from Korea sent me a fax. The fax stated there was a job offer for me as a professor in the newly established Department of Security Engineering at Chungbuk University in Cheongju, Korea. However, I

Flüssigkeitsgemischen. Vergleich zwischen experimentellen und berechneten Werten. Chem.-Ing.-Techn. 60(1988), 124 - 125.
The short summary of the second publication can be found in http://www3.interscience.wiley.com/cgi-bin/abstact/107603551/ABSTRACT: **Dr. Myeong-Hwan Choe, Prof. Dr. Hans-Georg Schecker:** *Flammpunkte von polynären Flüssigkeitsgemischen - Vergleich zwischen experimentellen und berechneten Werten,* Arbeitsgruppe Physikalisch-chemische Verfahrenstechnik des Fachbereiches Chemietechnik der Univ. Dortmund, Postfach 500 500, 4600 Dortmund 50 (Chemie Ingenieur Technik, Volume 60, Issue 2 , Seite 124 – 125)

4) http://www.chemietechnik.uni-dortmund.de/pcv/pcv-publs.htlm

immediately faxed him my rejection.

Prof. Schecker regretted my decision. Understandably, he had put in a lot of effort for me, and he had a father's heart for me. He had hoped that I would be a pioneer of security technology in Korea, but he respected my decision. I thank God for entrusting me with such a doctoral supervisor.

I received my doctorate on June 10, 1986. That day, in keeping with the tradition of the research group, I planted a pear tree next to the chemistry laboratory. A colleague got a lab dolly he had decorated with colorful papers and drove me a short distance. We had a little party in the research group.

I give glory to God. I thank Professor Schecker and Professor Bo-Sung Rhee. I would also like to thank the coworkers in Prof. Schecker's research group for their friendship and wholehearted help.

I applied to companies near Dortmund. At that time, German companies were reluctant to hire foreigners, so I received many rejections. Dr. Schecker had warned me about this beforehand. Furthermore, I wasn't fluent in German and didn't have the necessary professional skills that a German company might need. Therefore, it was difficult to find a job.

However, I have never regretted my decision to stay in Germany. Just as the Puritans initially struggled when they came to America, it was only natural that, as a pioneer of student missions in Germany, I had difficulty finding a job. But I saw Germany as my new home and wanted to live a life where I could share God's blessings with the Germans.

My sons, Stephan and Timothée, studied economics at the University of Bochum and both got good jobs and now work in Germany and the USA.

Ninth Story: Coworkers for the Studentenmission in Dortmund

"I am the good shepherd; I know my sheep and my sheep know me—just as the Father knows me and I know the Father—and I lay down my life for the sheep. I have other sheep that are not of this sheep pen. I must bring them also. They too will listen to my voice, and there shall be one flock and one shepherd."
(John 10:14-16)

1. German, Indonesian, and Korean students who worked for the Student Mission in Dortmund (1979-1986)

⋆ Adi Satria invited Iman Subagio, and Iman Martin Nachtrodt

Adi was a chemical engineering student from Indonesia. At the university cafeteria, he was invited by Sara Oh to Sunday worship on January 7, 1979. He came to the Sunday worship on January 21st with Kornelius(Iman), one of his compatriots who had been looking for a Bible-believing church. A week later, Kornelius led Martin Nachtrodt, a chemical engineering student, to the Sunday worship. Martin had a heart for foreign students.

In February 1979, Adi accepted God's call to be the distributor of divine blessings based on Genesis 12:2. The nationwide May conference took place from May 25th to 27th, 1979, in Bad Hönningen. Iman, Adi, and Korean missionaries from Dortmund took part.

Adi presented his belief with the title "A New Change," and Iman, "The People Need God's Word"(Luke 5). In a certain sense, Adi, like Abraham, played an important role in the divine work of redemption in Dortmund. Adi and Kornelius worked with us for the Gospel for about two years.

In my 1980 calendar book I can find names of those whom Sara Oh helped: Detlef, Mattina, Adi, Sook-Bin, Young-Hee, Hee-Sook, Gaby, and Theo.

⋆ Martin Nachtrodt: a friendly Christian

Martin Nachtrodt came to our Sunday worship on January 28 at the invitation of Kornelius. He had worked with the SMD(Student Mission in Deutschland), a sister group of Inter-Varsity-Fellowship. He was humble and friendly. He had grown up in a Christian family. One of his uncles had been a missionary abroad. He had a big heart for foreign students. At that time, he was helping an Afghan student couple named Hasan and Sadroldin. The couple was already Christian.

Martin Nachtrodt preached Luke 5:9-10 at the Open Bible Evening on June 21, 1979. On this Bible Evening, he accepted the divine calling for student mission.

He graduated from the university in July 1979 and wanted to

look for a job. He was already engaged to Marianne. He took part in the summer conference that took place from August 23 to 26, 1979, at the YMCA "Bundeshöhe" in Düsseldorf, and he confessed that he accepted the divine calling as a shepherd of students based on Rev. 1:7. We prayed that God might give him a PhD-course and an assistant position together, for example, at the Bible conference on January 29, 1980. By God's grace, he got an assistant position at the University of Dortmund and also received the doctorate course. He invited the students, like Matthias and Winfried, to study the Bible and to believe in Jesus.

On May 3, 1980, he married Marianne, who completed her internship as a teacher after finishing her studies. Esther, Abraham Lee, I, and some of our church attended their wedding in his hometown and congratulated them. It was a happy, traditional wedding celebration in the small village.

He received his doctorate in 1986 from the Chemical Engineering Department of the University of Dortmund. Since 1992, he has been a professor in the Applied Sciences Department of the Düsseldorf University, specializing in mechanical and process engineering. There he continues to work actively to lead students to faith in Jesus Christ.

⋆ Ludger Sickelmann and the 1st Dortmund Bible School

In mid-June 1979, I met a blond physics student named Ludger Sickelmann on the tram from Dortmund city to Dortmund-Barop and invited him to our Bible School. On the evening of June 20th and-21st(Wed-Thurs), 1979, we held a Bible School in our house church that we called the "Bible Academy".

However, on the first evening, none of the invited students came. So instead of holding the Bible School, we went to the dormitories and invited the students again. We also met Ludger, who lived in the dormitory at Ostenbergstraße 99, and invited him to the Bible School the next day. Ludger came to our Bible School on Thursday.

On Thursday evening, Martin Nachtrodt preached God's Word according to Luke 5:10. Martin R., our neighbor, and Detlef Hauerkampf were also there. Some of the students who attended this Bible School became important figures as they shared the blessings they had received from God over the years with many people.

After this Bible School, Detlef Hauerkamp personally learned the Bible with Sara Oh from June 23, 1979. Detlef paid attention to hygiene and always brought his own fork.

On July 12th of the same year, Ludger began studying the Gospel of John with me.

Martin R., our neighbor, was already studying the Bible with Esther every week.

Ludger took part in the summer conference in Düsseldorf from 23 to 26 August 1979 and testified to the grace of God because he had accepted the promise "From now on you shall be called Cephas" based on John 1:42. 'Cephas' means 'rock.' Ludger said he believed God would use him like "a rock" in God's work. He has since helped students with their Bible study and led many of them to the faith.

From August 11 to 20, 1982, Ludger and I, along with Vera Wunderlich, Sigrid Marquitan, Volker Keller, Daniel Park, Sarah Ki-Hyang Lee, and Abraham Lee from Cologne, took part in the Bible conference near Niagara Falls in Canada.

Ludger served God faithfully and helped many students, such as Walter Nett, Winfried Schmidt, Di, and others, with their Bible studies and with good advice. God blessed his devotion abundantly, so that the students met God personally and became blessings to others.

On Sunday, March 18, 1984, we sent Ludger to Cologne with a prayer so that he could do an internship there to become a full-time Gospel worker. In Cologne, too, Ludger dedicated himself to the Lord for the Gospel.

From the winter semester of 1985/86, Ludger studied communications engineering at the College of Applied Sciences in Krefeld. There, too, he eagerly helped students through individual Bible studies.

⋆ Karl-Heinz Hohmann

The 1981 summer conference took place from August 27th to 30th, 1981, at Naumburg Castle near Frankfurt am Rhein. Before that, we visited student residences and invited the students to this conference. One day before this conference, Sara Oh met Karl-Heinz Hohmann in the dormitory and began praying for him. Then, on September 4th of the same year, he began studying the Bible with her and also started attending Sunday worship at church. He was born in 1956. He had written good essays in middle and high school. He liked classical music and biology. In particular, he had a linguistic talent for Turkish. He completed his studies in pedagogy on July 1, 1982, at the College of Education in Dortmund. On December 31, 1981, he moved into a small room next to the entrance of our house church on Baroper Bahnhofstrasse and lived there for about a year. Then he moved to a room in the apartment of Paul and Sara Chang on "Am Heiligen Busch."

⋆ Walter Nett

In mid-November 1981, Ludger said he was praying for students who wanted to learn God's Word. God quickly answered his prayer. On Saturday, November 21, 1981, Ludger and Esther invited a computer science student named Walter Nett from the dormitory on Stockumerstraße.

Walter began studying the Gospel of Mark with Ludger. The surname "Nett" means "friendly," and he was a friendly, smart student. He was good at memorizing and was faithful, courageously following the teachings of Jesus. Through studying the Bible in Luke 5, he learned of the calling of Simon Peter. After Jesus got into Peter's fishing boat and taught the Word of God to the crowd on the beach, he said to Simon Peter, "Go where it's deep and throw out the net!"

At Jesus' word, Peter cast out the net and caught many fish. Jesus said to Peter, who bowed down before Him, "Do not be afraid. From now on, you will catch people! "

Based on this Bible verse, Walter accepted God's calling as a fisher of men to save people.

At the conference on June 29, 1982, Walter said that he would raise 12 student apostles, just as Jesus raised 12 apostles and brought the good news of eternal life to the world. Walter completed his studies in the summer of 1982 with the degree Dipl.-Ing. in computer science. He wanted to help students in Dortmund believe in Jesus Christ and live as disciples of Jesus. That is why he took a part-time assistant job at the Distance-Learning University of Hagen, the neighboring city of Dortmund.

In 1982, he helped Gerd Franken (4 semesters of computer science), Reiner Stahlhut(6 semesters of statistics), and Reiner(6 semesters of economics) with the Bible study.

Abraham Lee in Cologne suggested that Walter move to Cologne and be promoted as a future church leader. He accepted the proposal as a divine calling and moved to Cologne in mid-1983.

He married the cheerful Wynelle and raised their children well. This family is happy and brings joy to many people.

Walter took over the leadership and preaching post in the Cologne Student Church from Abraham Lee. After many years as a church leader in Cologne, he handed over the leadership to Eberhard Gross and moved with his family to Mönchengladbach. Eberhard is the husband of Ulrike Gross, who was sent out from our church in Bochum. Eberhard came to the Cologne Church after seeing the inviting poster that Andreas Schmeinck had put up.

⋆ Di & El

In early March 1982, Ludger and Esther invited Di, a seventh-semester chemical engineering student, to study the Bible. His fiancée, El, began studying the Bible with Esther on October 22 of the same year. Di was a relaxed person, and El had a fine sense of humor. The two got along very well as a couple. Their wedding took place in the church in Duisburg they had attended. We were at her wedding. After the Wedding Worship, young friends of the church congratulated the couple with various celebration programs.

El learned the Bible from Esther, and in September 1983, based on the Words Mark 3:13-15, she accepted God's call to missionary work with young people. She actively helped students and young people through Bible study.

On April 7, 1984, Di shared about his faith experience in our church. When he was little, his family prayed before bed. As a child he was relatively passive. At the age of 18, he began attending church in his hometown. However, he was afraid of the changes in his life. He was also reluctant to pray aloud. But little by little he learned to pray there. He then attended the University of Dortmund and lived in a student dormitory. Ludger invited him to study the Bible, and through Bible study he learned to live in trust in the Lord. Di and El did their best to work with us to lead students and young people to faith in the Gospel through Bible study.

After graduating from university, Di got a job at a company in another city, and the couple moved there.

⋆ Correction of my sermon

Around June 1979, I asked a German student named Juttah, who was sitting at the entrance to the cafeteria at the University of Dortmund, to correct my German message. She corrected the message and returned it to me, saying that it was not good to call the students "sheep." She was right. Humans are not animals. Through this incident, I learned to understand the language and feelings of students who do not yet believe in God.

⋆ Jericho March to the University of Bochum

On Saturday, November 24, 1979, we, coworkers in Dortmund, walked from our church in Dortmund-Barop to the University of Bochum and back. The distance from our church to the University of Bochum is approximately 20 km. We called this march "Jericho March" because we wanted to open the hearts of the students in Bochum to the Gospel. The Old Testament reports that when the Israelites marched around the walls of Jericho for seven days, the walls of Jericho fell. During this march, we believed that the hearts of the students in Bochum would be opened, that they would learn God's Word and accept Jesus. And this actually happened later. Many students, like Hartmut and Renate, opened their hearts and worked with us for the student mission.

2. Korean Missionaries, Who Worked in Dortmund

I have already written something about You-Kang Cho and Sara Oh, who had worked for the student mission in Essen, Bochum, and Dortmund since 1978.

On April 4, 1979, You-Kang Hur(married to Cho) returned to Korea and began working for the student mission of the Seoul National University with her husband, Seong-Gi Cho.

Now I would like to tell you about the student missionaries in Dortmund.

I came to Germany with a student visa. As mentioned earlier, the Korean government did not allow self-financed study abroad at the time to save foreign currency such as dollars. In order to obtain a passport for studying and coming to Germany, I had to present an invitation letter and a financial guarantee certificate from my doctoral supervisor to the passport department in Seoul. Since I was married to Esther, I could have come to Germany for the purpose of family reunification. However, God had a different plan. At the invitation of my doctoral supervisor, I came to Germany as a student. And I had to meet various conditions to get the passport, so I was able to figure out how to obtain it to study abroad. Later, I was able to help the Korean brothers and sisters in faith to come to Germany as student missionaries.

In fact, neither Esther nor I, nor Sarah Ki-Hyang Lee, had any intention of inviting any more student missionaries from Korea to Germany. Sarah Lee and Esther had learned through my letter that Professor Bo-Sung Rhee, who had been my master's supervisor, was staying at the University of Dortmund. Prof. Rhee introduced them to Prof. Schecker as my Ph.D. supervisor. Prof. Schecker wrote me a letter of invitation that included the financial guarantee. That's why I started applying for a passport to come to Germany as a student.

After I arrived in Germany, I realized that our fellow believers in Korea could also come to Germany as student missionaries. Sara Oh(married to Chang) and I visited Peter Kornowski, Young-Hee(영희) Kornowski's husband, who explained the legal situation in Korea, and asked him to write an invitation letter for Andreas Ahn. He kindly wrote an invitation letter for him. Soon-Ki Yoon(윤순기) and I visited Dr. Werner Sasse in the East Asia Department of the University of Bochum and asked him to write an invitation letter for Paula Kim. Esther and I asked Dr. Walter Reichert in Rheda to write an invitation for Rebecca Son. I gave each inviting person a written statement that I remained responsible for the financial affairs of the invitee. We then sent the invitation letters to Korea, so that student missionaries would come to Germany.

On the other hand, Peter Suh in Daejeon, South Korea, had encouraged university graduates from his church to fly to Germany as student missionaries. This is how God's work of student mission in Germany began. Most Korean missionaries in Germany today were originally student missionaries.

Around the 1988 Olympic Games in Seoul, the law in Korea was changed so that one could study abroad at one's own expense. Around 1990, God expanded His worldwide missionary work to Hungary, Russia, and other former communist countries through our Korean student missionaries.

Mission work by student missionaries is an effective method because the missionaries can first learn the language of the country through language courses and university studies, learn about the culture of the country, and do their missionary work effectively.

God blessed the German mission first through nurse missionaries and then through student missionaries. That's why we honor God. God's wisdom is wonderful.

⋆ Missionaries and Their Bible Study Friends

Andreas Ahn(Jae-Ryong Ahn/안재룡) arrived in Dortmund at the beginning of April 1979.

We didn't know when Andreas Ahn would come to Germany. He arrived at Düsseldorf Airport on a Sunday in April, called us, and asked how he could get to Dortmund. I replied in mixed German and Korean that he should take the train to Dortmund Central Station and then come to us by taxi. He then took a taxi from the airport to us and had to pay around 100 marks for it. He probably misunderstood my mixed language.

There was no German course at the University of Dortmund. That's why he had to attend the German course at the University of Bochum. To travel from Dortmund to the University of

Bochum using public transport, he had to buy three tickets at that time: one ticket for the tram to Dortmund Central Station, a second ticket for the train to Bochum Central Station, and a third ticket for the tram to Bochum University. To save on travel costs, Andreas Ahn rode his bike to the language course at the University of Bochum. The distance from Dortmund-Barop to the University of Bochum is approximately 20 km, and it takes around 40 minutes by bike.

Andreas Ahn could have worked as an architect in Korea and led a successful life if he had only wanted to. However, he lived in poverty because he wanted to work as a student missionary to bring the good news of Jesus Christ to German students. Although he initially could not speak German, he actively invited students, for example, Felix, to study the Bible. Felix came from Stephanstraße in the city of Kreuztal. I remember his street because his street is my first name.

Andreas Ahn helped other students such as Arnold(from June 1979), Ki-Seok Baek(백기석), Kurt, Se-Ja(세야), Seon-Ok Baek(백선옥), Seok-Ryun Kim(김석련), Do-Sil Kim(김도실, from March 1980), Winfried(from June 1980), Rainer, and others with the Bible study.

Ruth Ahn(Korean name: Young-Gee Yoon/윤영기), Andreas Ahn's wife, arrived on Thursday, February 12, 1981, with her first son, Johann. At the Sunday worship on February 24, she presented her testimony as follows:

When she hadn't visited our church in Korea, she didn't know what to live for. When her good plans failed, she was very disappointed. But in the spring of 1971, she met Jesus personally through a Bible study of the Gospel of Mark and Genesis. The Bible taught her that the real purpose of life is to save the people of the world through the Gospel. She then experienced her personal redemption through the study of the Romans, accepting God's love and loving God instead of loving any creature. Through Genesis 12:2, she accepted God's promise that He would use her and her family as a stream of blessings for many people. In fact, through this family, God led many students in Germany to faith.

Andreas Ahn worked as an architect in Cologne alongside his university studies. His family moved to Cologne on June 26, 1982. This family led several students in Cologne to faith and helped them live as disciples of Jesus.

On July 15, 1986, Andreas completed his master's degree at the University of Dortmund and began his doctoral studies at the Technical University of Aachen.

In 1987 his family moved to Aachen and worked for the student mission at the Technical University Aachen. The Ahn family helped the TU students, such as Werner Theisen and Guido Wilms, with Bible studies so that they could meet Jesus personally. These two individuals worked with the Ahn family for the student mission there. Andreas's first son, Johann, studied medicine at the TU Aachen, became a specialist, and now works in Berlin. Their second son, Maga, is also faithful to Jesus Christ.

Sara Oh(요현금) flew to Korea on April 2, 1980, married **Paul Chang**(장두진), and returned to Germany on May 7, 1980. Sara Chang gave birth to her first baby, Mira, in October 1982, and later to her second baby, Hanpol. We thanked God for their babies.

Dong-Ok Park(박동옥) and **Doo-Gyoo Kim**(김두규). Dong-Ok had worked together as a nurse and missionary in Rheda with Esther. Dong-Ok and Doo-Gyoo moved to Dortmund on April 21, 1980, and worked with us for the German student mission. For this purpose, Dong-Ok Kim got a job at Mary's Hospital in Dortmund-Homburg. Her daughter, Hae-Jin(해진), was one year old when they moved. After that, a boy named Woo-Jin(우진) was born to them. Doo-Gyoo Kim has a talent for telling interesting stories, so we all laughed out loud when he shared them. The couple currently lives in Essen.

Paula Kim(Sah-Hyon Lee/이사현) arrived from Daegu(대구), Korea, on Sunday, March 23, 1980. After the Sunday service, we welcomed her at Düsseldorf Airport. I first met her in December 1976 at a conference in Daejeon, Korea. She had actually wanted to come in the spring of 1979, but she worked as a teacher for about a year before came to Germany. She kissed the floor of the Forum Square of the University of Bochum because she considered it to be her Holy Land. She brought only DM 1,000 from Korea, but she trusted in God and worked for her living expenses.

She married Joseph Kim in October 1983 in Daegu, Korea.

She wrote me a letter on October 5. In it, she wrote about her marriage: "I trust everything in God, who has led me to the best path so far and who will continue to guide me to the best path in the future."

God has richly blessed her trust in Him.

Joseph Kim(Bong-Ki Kim/김봉기), Paula's husband, arrived in Germany in mid-March 1986. At his first Sunday worship in Dortmund on March 16, he expressed what he was praying for:

He wants to serve God as a Bible teacher and prayer servant. In addition, he aimed to master German in one year, receive his doctorate in about four years, raise three full-time shepherds and three devoted, pious servants like Mary, and open England to the Gospel in ten years.

This couple first lived in Dortmund and then in Bochum, helping Renate Buchholz(married to Schmeinck) and Ulrike Brinkmann(married to Gross) with the Bible study.

Joseph Kim received his doctorate in history from the University of Bochum. He wrote his dissertation, "John Dewey and China: The Importance of His Social Theory for Intercultural Communication."[5)]

The couple currently works in Duisburg and plans to open a school in North Korea. Samuel Kim, the couple's first child, earned a master's degree from Harvard University and married.

---

5) Kim, Bongki, "John Dewey and China: The Importance of His Social Theory for Intercultural Communication," dissertation summary: see www.uni-duisburg.de/Institute/OAWISS/download/doc/paper19.doc

The couple has two children, and currently works in Korea. Joseph Kim's daughter, Johanna Kim, is a medical doctor.

Rebecca Han(Jang-Won Son/손장원) arrived in Germany on Wednesday, June 25, 1980. On that day in 1950, the Korean War broke out between North and South Korea. She did not come to Germany as a messenger of war but as a messenger of peace. She had studied Korean up to a master's degree in Korea. After completing her four-year bachelor's degree, she worked for a few years as a schoolteacher and then as a research assistant at Chungnam University. However, she truly wanted to work actively for the mission as a lay missionary abroad. Because she had studied Korean, she had little opportunity to go abroad as a lay missionary. But God opened the mission door for her to come to Germany as a student missionary and study at the East Asia Department of the University of Bochum. Rebecca Han flew to Korea on July 23, 1982, and married Joseph Han. After the marriage, she returned to Germany on September 29, 1982.

A year later, **Joseph Han**(Sang-Dae Han/한상대) arrived in Germany on their wedding day, August 14, 1983. With his arrival, a new era of missionary life began for both of them. Although he had studied electrical engineering in Korea, he began to study spatial planning at the University of Dortmund and completed it in five years, earning the Dipl. Ing., which corresponds to the bachelor's plus master's degree. He faithfully fulfilled his three roles as a missionary, student, and householder. Their two children, Maria and Johann, were well educated. Maria is now a medical doctor, and Johann works in Berlin. During his studies, Joseph Han sold newspapers in the evenings and faithfully helped students with Bible study. Nevertheless, he successfully completed his studies in spatial planning. God blessed his simple faith in Him and his devoted support of Rebecca.

After completing his studies, Joseph Han got a job at a bank in Frankfurt. This is why the family moved to Darmstadt and opened a new student church there. The couple helped Manfred with a Bible study. Manfred had doubted God, but with the help of both, he overcame his doubts. He married Tanja from Moldova and has four children.

After Joseph Han passed away in 2010, Manfred took over the leadership of the church and the ministry. He later moved with his family to a free evangelical church.

I remember well the friendly face of Rebecca's mother, who fell asleep in June 2021. She had begun the work of blessing in her family. Rebecca Han took over her blessing work and continues it by passing on the divine blessing to numerous people in Germany and around the world.

Jesaja Lee(Tack-Yong Lee/이택용) arrived in Germany on October 15, 1980. After graduating from Seoul National University in Korea, he worked for several years as a researcher at an institute in Daejeon, Korea. However, he gave up his well-paid job and came to Dortmund as a student missionary to lead students and people to the faith. His wife, **Bekkie Lee**, joined him on November 5, 1981.

A few years later, Mark Yang of Anam UBF, who had sent Jesaja and Bekkie Lee as missionaries, attended the summer conference in Germany. He suggested to Jesaja that he should stop living the hard life of a student missionary, return to Korea, and work with him. Jesaja replied that once he was sent out as a missionary, he would like to live his whole life as a missionary.

On July 12, 1987, a farewell Sunday worship for my family and the family of Joseph and Paula Kim as pioneers of the University of Bochum took place in the Dortmund church. At this service, Bekkie Lee testified to the grace of God in her life, using Romans 1:1-5 as her key verse:

"I grew up in a very happy Christian family. When I failed the Seoul National University entrance exam in 1970, I made an oath that I would live for God when I passed the next Seoul National University entrance exam. And God answered that prayer. After my entrance to the Seoul National University, I studied the Bible in Genesis 1:31 at Jongno UBF, realized my sin of having lived for people up until then, and received great grace. After that, according to Jesus' words in John 21:15, 'Do you love me?,' I accepted Jesus' love and mission and became a missionary."

This missionary couple helped Joseph Schulte, Ralf Nau, Hans-Peter Fick, Viola, Beate König, and Johannes Honschopp with the Bible study to live as disciples of Jesus.

When I moved to Bochum, Jesaja Lee took over the leadership and preaching office of the Dortmund church, and the couple served the Lord faithfully in their church.

Rebekka Lee(Ki-Min Lee/이기민) arrived in Dortmund on October 13, 1982. During her high school days, she had already studied the Bible with Ruth Ahn, who had been a teacher at her school. Rebekka studied nursing at the University of Chungnam for four years and then came to Dortmund as a student missionary. After about two years, Rebekka studied medicine in Düsseldorf.

Tenth Story: God's Work in Dortmund through Bible Study

"I am the good shepherd; I know my sheep and my sheep know me— just as the Father knows me and I know the Father—and I lay down my life for the sheep. I have other sheep that are not of this sheep pen. I must bring them also. They too will listen to my voice, and there shall be one flock and one shepherd."
(John 10:14-16)

1. God's Work during the Time of the House Church at Ostenbergstraße 22 (August 15, 1978 – September 26, 1981)

⋆ Sook-Bin Lee(이숙빈) and Eun-Ja Kim(김언자)

Sook-Bin Lee, a Korean who studied violin at the Folkwang Music College in Essen, began coming to our church for Sunday worship in the spring of 1979 at the invitation of Sara Oh(Chang) and attended the summer conference. She faithfully attended our Sunday worship for about two years and learned the Bible from Sara Oh.

She once said about the relationship between musical talent and practice, "If you want to be an excellent violin player, you should have a talent for playing the violin and practice well. I don't have this excellent talent, but I practice diligently."

I think she said that out of modesty. After graduating, she became a professor in Seoul.

In August 1979, Esther's cousin Eun-Ja Kim, who was taking a doctoral course in French literature in Paris, visited us for about a month. During this time, she attended a German course in Dortmund and studied the Bible with Esther. After completing her doctorate, she worked as a professor of French literature at Kangwon National University in Chuncheon. She also served as president of the French Language Society in South Korea, thus contributing to the promotion of French literature in Korea.

⋆ Martin R., a Good Business Student

In late May 1979, Esther began praying for Martin, who lived in the apartment next door to ours. He was a diligent business student and a devout and socially engaged Catholic. Esther taught him the Bible once a week, and I looked after little Stephan. My calendar book from June 21, 1979, notes that he learned the power of rebirth through Chapter 3 of the Gospel of John.

He completed his five years of studies in early 1980. Today, he works as a board member of a well-known company.

⋆ Summer Conference 1979

The West German Summer Conference 1979 took place in

Düsseldorf from August 23 to 26. From Dortmund, Martin Nachtrodt, Ludger, Adi, Sook-Bin Lee, Ki-Seok Baek(백기석, a student at the University of Bochum, invited by Andreas Ahn), Seok-Ryun Kim(김석련), and Dong-Ok Kim and her husband Doo-Gyoo Kim, Bok-Eum Kim(김복음), Sara Oh, Andreas Ahn, Esther, and I participated in the conference.

At this conference, Martin Nachtrodt gave a testimony stating that he accepted God's calling as shepherd and Bible teacher for the students.

⋆ Bernhard & Christian Kommendera (from October 1980)

When Rebecca Son arrived in Germany, she had the courage to soon invite students to study the Bible. In October 1980, she invited a theology student named Bernhard Kommendera from the University of Bochum to study the Bible. He introduced us to Christian, his older brother, who studied geology in Bochum. The two brothers participated in the autumn Bible conference in Hagen from November 7 to 9, 1980. From January 1981, Bernhard studied Genesis with Rebecca Son. In March 1981, he said that with the first words of the Bible, "In the beginning, God created heaven and earth," he changed his mindset from self-centered to God-centered. He then flew to England around September of that year to continue his theology studies at Cambridge University.

Christian Kommendera also began studying the Bible with Paula Kim in early January 1981 and continued until 1985. He was faithful and had a pure heart.

⋆ Wedding of Martin Nachtrodt, exploration of the universities of Hanover and Hamburg, and participation in the US Conference

At the Sunday worship on March 2, 1980, we thanked God for Martin Nachtrodt's doctorate course. Martin married Marianne on Saturday, May 3, of that year, in his hometown of Warburg. We, Abraham Lee from Cologne, and some of our missionaries, attended this wedding. It was a traditional wedding. After the wedding ceremony in the village church, a procession followed the bride and groom to the banquet hall, with children scattering flower petals along the way. Many relatives and neighbors of the bride and groom were present, making it a blessed and happy wedding.

May 15, 1980, was Ascension Day, a public holiday. Esther and I drove with our then one-year-and-three-month-old son Siseong(지성), later renamed Stephan when he received German citizenship), to the universities of Hanover and Hamburg to explore these universities with the intent to eventually begin evangelism among students there. Stephan could walk a little at this point.

The University of Hanover was the first university in Germany to help shape the industrial revolution. It is also one of the oldest technical universities in Germany, and its university library is one of the most significant technical libraries in the country.

At the end of June of that year, I visited Kurie Park, a nurse missionary in Berlin. After all the missionaries in Berlin had moved to West Germany, she remained alone in Berlin. I suggested that she move to Dortmund if she wanted, but she said she would stay in Berlin. After visiting her, I toured the Free University of Berlin and the Berlin Zoo before returning.

From Wednesday, July 30, to Monday, August 11, 1980, Abraham Lee, Volker Keller, Sigrid Marquitan, Isaak Yook(육이삭), Ludger Sickelman, and I visited the United States to participate in the Niagara Summer Conference in Canada. Tim Brauns and Andy Griffin were key student leaders of Chicago UBF at the time. The two preached on the Way of the Cross according to the Gospel of Mark, chapters 8 and 9. The conference ended on Sunday.

Missionaries from New York drove our German mission team to New York and Washington, where we visited the Empire State Building, the White House, the Capitol, and the Lincoln Memorial.

⋆ The First Dortmund Conference in Hagen

From November 7 to 9, 1980, the first historical Bible Conference of the Dortmund Student Church took place at the Youth Hotel in Hagen, with Ludger Sickelmann, Sara Oh, and Andreas Ahn preaching. These three individuals were very important to our church at the time: Ludger, a German Bible teacher; Sara, a nurse missionary; and Andreas, a student missionary.

Bernhard Kommendera, Christian Kommendera, and Martin(theology student at the University of Bochum) participated in this conference along with our missionaries.

Young-Sook Kang(강영숙) from Frankfurt and Hwa-Soon Lee(이화순) from Stuttgart also participated in this conference and supported us. After the conference, Christian and Bernhard, Kommendera's brothers, began one-to-one Bible studies with Paula Lee and Rebecca Son, respectively.

A week later, from November 14 to 16, the Stuttgart Bible Conference took place in the Tübingen Youth Hotel, which I attended. It was a cool day, but there was no heating, so I had to wear a coat during the conference. A week prior, however, at the Dortmund Conference at the Hagen Youth Hotel, it was warm thanks to the heating. I realized that the people in Baden-Württemberg had become rich through frugal living.

⋆ List of Bible Friends 1980

Here is a list of students who came to study the Bible or were on our prayer list in 1980:

- **Sara Oh**: Detlef, Mattina, Adi, Sook-Bin Lee(이숙빈), Young-Hee Kornowski, Hee-Sook Kim(김희숙), Gaby, Theo
- **Esther Choe**: Martin R., Dong-Ok, Gaby, Birgit, Marianne, Mrs. Kern Irmgard in Hagen, Naziba,
- **Bok-Eum Lee**: Seon-Ok Baek(백선옥), Barbara
- **Dong-Ok Park**: Ellinor Pfützner, Purin, Grandpa Reichert in Rheda
- **Stephan Choe**: Martin Nachtrodt, Ludger, Felix, Kornelius, Doo-Kyoo Kim, Peter K., Soon-Ki Yoon(윤순기), Soo-Pyung Kim(김수평)
- **Martin N.**: Matthias, Winfried, Hasan, Sadroldin
- **Ludger Sickelmann**: Joseph(accepted John 1:14, prayed as a shepherd candidate), Eckardt, Helmut, Geo, his father, his sister Christel, Armin
- **Andreas Ahn**: Rainer(John's Gospel), Arnold, Markus, Ki-Suk(기석), Kwang-Sung Kim(김광성), Do-Sil Kim(김도실), Winfried, Felix
- **Paula Lee**(from March 23, 1980): Sohan, Winfried, Tina, Helga
- **Rebecca Son**(from June 25, 1980): Margaret, Ulrike, Usla(Mark's Gospel), Birgit
- **Jesaja Lee**(from October 15, 1980): Ali, Sabine, Petra

⋆ Winfried Schmidz

On January 16, 1981, he began studying Genesis with Ludger. At that time, he was in his third year of studying physics and living in the Baroperstraße student dormitory. He had attended a Catholic gymnasium taught by monks. At that time, physics in Germany was considered a subject that encompassed both natural sciences and engineering. It is no coincidence that many

German physicists were awarded the Nobel Prize.

Winfried was friendly and kind. For about nine months, he studied the Bible with Ludger every week and became friends with us.

⋆ Bible Friends 1981

- **Ludger Sickelmann**: Winfried Schmitz, Armin, Usla, Britta, Fritz, Bodo Piller, Walter
- **Rebecca Son**: Bernhard Kommendera, Birgit(lived in the same dormitory as Rebecca in Bochum, Electrical Engineering 1st semester), Britta
- **Paula Kim**: Christian Kommendera
- **Esther Choe**: Martin R., Andreas Holzmann, Birgit Volker(Jan. 23 ~ Sep. 5, 1981), Christian Hubertz(July 23 ~ Nov. 11, 1981. Gospel of Luke. & Mark), Michael Nitze, Giesla Kaiser(Jan. 8, 1981 ~ Nov. 30, 1982)
- **Sara Chang**: Sook-Bin Lee(이숙빈), Markus, Michael, Hugo, Dorothea, Theo
- **Jesaja Lee**: Josef Schulte, Jürgen, Petra, Sabine, Georg
- **Andreas Ahn**: Felix, Winfried Sagola
- **Stephan Choe**: Martin Nachtrodt, Dietrich, Udo, Buckard, Klaus
- **Paul Chang**: Christian, Winfried

2. God's Work during the Time of the House Church at Baroper Bahnhofstraße 73 (September 26, 1981 – May 31, 1984)

⋆ New Bible Friends During the Time at Baroper Bahnhofstraße 73

Our house church at Ostenbergstr. 22 was too small for the coworkers. Therefore, on Saturday, September 26, 1981, we moved to Baroper Bahnhofstraße 73.

After the move, I spent eleven days at the Dortmund City Hospital, from Monday, September 28, to Thursday, October 8, where I underwent surgery for an otitis media. However, on Sunday, October 4, I was able to attend the Sunday worship with the doctor's permission and preach.

From October 30 to November 1, 1981, we held a Fall Conference at the Hagen Youth Hostel with the theme "Repent and Believe in the Gospel!"

Missionary Hwa-Soon Lee(이화순) came from Stuttgart to strengthen us.

The preachers were Ludger(Friday evening), Ruth Ahn(before breakfast on Saturday), Joseph Schulte(Saturday morning), Andreas Ahn(Saturday evening), Jesaja Lee(Sunday morning), and Karl-Heinz Hohmann(Sunday morning).

On Sunday, November 15, 1981, we celebrated the Dedication Worship of the new House Bible Church. On that day, we prayed that twelve good Bible teachers like Moses would grow up here. During this worship, three members of our church shared their testimonies of faith. These three coworkers were, in a sense, three pioneers of the faith: Ludger as a German Bible teacher; Andreas Ahn as a student missionary; and Sara Chang is as a nurse missionary.

Based on Mark 5:36, Ludger said he repented out of fear because he did not believe in the power of God and would now serve God joyfully in faith.

Andreas Ahn said he had found faith in the Creator God through studying Genesis with Nam-Sik Woo(우남식) in Korea. He had wanted to live for the glory of Korea, but he desired to live and work joyfully for the glory of God.

Sara Chang said she found faith in God after 1975 through Bible study with Yang-Nim Hwang(황양님). She never hated sin, but now she would hate sin and love righteousness.

At the end of the year, we began to pray for the students at 263 universities and colleges in Germany and for all people in 164 countries around the world that they would believe in God.

⋆ Joseph Schulte

Jesaja Lee began praying for Joseph Schulte in September 1981. Joseph lived in Sundern, a village in the Sauerland, and drove to the university by car. At the beginning of February 1982, he began studying Romans with Jesaja. He studied the Word of God for about a year and also attended the Summer Bible Conference at Naumburg Castle from August 26 to 29, 1982. Jesaja and I visited his home in Sundern in 1982. His parents' house was in a beautiful area and owned a restaurant, which Josseph later took it over.

⋆ **Ralf Nau**

On October 19, 1982, Jesaja Lee invited Ralf Nau, a third-semester computer science student, to study the Bible. Ralf lived in Ennepetal and already believed in God. At the beginning of November 1982, he began studying the Gospel of John with Jesaja Lee. In July of the following year, he said he wanted to invite students to study the Bible with Jesaja Lee. At the summer conference from August 15 to 18, 1983, he made his faith in Jesus Christ known through his testimony. He studied the Bible with Jesaja until the spring of 1985.

⋆ **Karl-Heinz Hohmann**

He helped Hein Brase, Peter Grafschicke, Rainer Hartmann(Electrical Engineering), Peter Wittler(Computer Science, 5th semester), Volker Oles(Ehemical Engineering, 7th semester), and others.

⋆ **Bible Students of Korean Missionaries**

In 1982, Korean missionaries also helped many students with Bible studies.

Sara Chang faithfully helped Karl-Heinz, Sook-Bin Lee, and Detlef. She also helped Dorothea Schulz(first semester of Physics & Music; her father was a pastor), Markus Theo, Wolfgang Liesegang, Sabine Bosdorf, Edith, Hugo(since the beginning of

December 1981), and Norbert Kaup(from June 1982 with the Gospel of John).

Paula Kim taught God's Word to Christian Kommendera and prayed that he would become a prayer warrior for the students in Bochum. In January 1982, while studying Genesis 1, Armin learned the order of values: firstly God, secondly people, and thirdly all other creatures. We call it "the Order of Creation."

Paula Kim also helped Herbert, Georg, Andreas Menschuk(3rd semester, Architecture), and Eva with the Bible study.

Rebecca Han helped theology student Bernhard Kommendera with God's Word in Genesis from March 5, 1982, so that he accepted the truth of a God-centered life. She also helped Britta with Genesis(from July 22, 1981), praying that she would become a prayer mother. On November 11, 1981, she helped Usla Wojciechowski with the Gospel of Mark, as well as Gabrielle, Ulrich, Petra(Special Education), and Jutta(Sports in the fourth semester).

Andreas Ahn helped Felix, Winfried Sagola, and Paul.

His wife, Ruth Ahn, helped Koreans such as Hee-Gi Kang(강희기), Doo-Gyoo Kim, and Hong-Soon Han(한홍순) in February 1981.

Martin R., whom **Esther Choe** taught the Bible, graduated from university and moved to another city after work. She then faithfully helped Schwester El with Bible study, beginning on

October 24, 1982.

From July 1983, Esther also helped Heidi Schwender, a medical assistant from Gevelsberg.

I helped Nian Kleff(February 1982), and from June, Thomas and Andreas Holtmann weekly through the Bible study. I also helped Ludger and Di through the Bible study.

⋆ Heidi(i.e., Heidemarie) Schwender

Heidi, a medical assistant from Gevelsberg, was invited by the Kommendera brothers and attended our church from the end of July 1983 to March 1984. She had a pure heart for God and studied Genesis and Romans with Esther.

⋆ Ulrich and Hans-Peter Fick

In early 1983, **Jesaja Lee** taught the Gospel of John to Ulrich, a mechanical engineering student, and Ulrich wrote his views on the passages faithfully.

At the end of October 1983, Jesaja Lee began to teach Hans-Peter Fick, whom Jonrad Jesaja had introduced to him, the Bible. Hans-Peter lived in Ennepetal and studied chemical engineering. For three years, he studied the Bible with Jesaja and faithfully served God with us in our church. In April 1986, instead of continuing his study of chemical engineering, he began an apprenticeship as a banker and subsequently worked successfully as a banker

⋆ **Lily Anggreny**

In March 1983, **Sara Chang** met Lily Anggreny in a student dormitory in Bochum and taught her the Bible several times. Lily was born in Indonesia to Chinese parents. Her parents are evangelical Christians.

She took part in the 1992 Paralympic Games of the Barcelona Olympics as a member of the German National Wheelchair Team and won gold medals in the 5000 m, as well as silver and bronze medals in other events.

⋆ **Hartmut Rose**

Hartmut Rose studied electrical engineering at the University of Bochum. In the summer of 1983, he was invited by **Jesaja Lee and Paula Kim**. He had studied the Bible with Bekkie Lee and attended Sunday worship several times at our church in Dortmund. After my family and the family of Joseph and Paula Kim moved to Bochum in March 1987 and began student ministry there, he studied the book of Romans with me in 1989 and confessed that Jesus had seen his faith and given him a new life for God. In his 1989 testimony of faith, he spoke about his progress in faith:

"I met my friend Peter and his parents when I was in high school. With their help, I realized that lying, stealing, and disobeying my parents were sins. I then confessed my moral sins to God, and felt a deep peace of mind. After that, I started attending church youth meetings. I found great joy there and led a youth group.

In the second semester of 1984(?) at the University of Bochum, I joined the Navigators. In the Navigators, I learned to read the Bible regularly with joy. Around June 1985(?), two young, black-haired women, Bekkie Lee and Paula Kim, invited me to Bible study and a conference. However, I turned down the invitations from Bekkie Lee and Jesaja Lee twice. After the third invitation, I attended the Sunday worship in Dortmund."

⋆ Ludger Sent to Cologne

On Sunday, March 18, 1984, we sent Ludger to Cologne with prayers because he wanted to receive full-time shepherd training there. Until then, Ludger had preached at student meetings every Tuesday evening. After he was sent to Cologne, Jesaja preached for a few months. On December 8 of that year, Di began preaching.

⋆ Other Bible Friends

Back then, we had one-to-one Bible studies with about 10 students per week. Rebecca Han taught the Gospel of John to Peter Müller, a third-year music and mathematics student, in the winter semester of 1982/83. Monika Würzinger was a fellow student of Paula Kim's. When Paula Kim invited her to the 1983 summer conference, God opened her heart to participate willingly. Monika also studied the Bible with Rebecca Han and accepted God's forgiveness and grace.

Because God was so gracious, Rolf also gladly participated in the summer Bible conference.

3. God's Work during the Time of the House Church at Helenenbergweg 7 (May 5, 1984 – Feb. 28, 1987)

⋆ **Bible Friends 1984**

The German coworkers in our church also actively invited students to the Bible study.

El helped Günter Tschirsch, a tenth-semester electrical engineering student, with the Bible study.

Heidi taught Genesis to Brunhilde.

Ralf Nau invited **Hans-Peter** to study the Bible. Ralf himself learned the Bible from Jesaja Lee or Bekkie Lee. Hans-Peter prayed to teach the students the Bible.

This year, around 10–15 students learned the Bible one to one per week.

A summer Bible conference for Germany took place from August 23 to 26(Thursday-Sunday), 1984. In addition to Korean missionaries, Di, El, Hans-Peter, Mostafa, and Ralf Wortmann(Bible friend of Joseph Hans) participated.

At this conference, **Hans-Peter** shared his testimony of faith under the title "The Love of God I Experienced during My Studies," based on John 3:16.

⋆ **The list of Bible Friends in 1984:**

- **Bekkie Lee**: Andree Bockholt(5th semester of Architecture, John's Gospel, starting in January), Hartmut Rose(starting from March 28), Mustafa(starting in mid-1984), Hans-Peter(he prayed to teach the Bible to others.)
- **Jesaja Lee**: Konrad Tschersich(starting at the beginning of the year), Ralf Nau(Romans), Ralf invited Hans-Peter.
- **Sara Chang**: Karl-Heinz(he was exempted from military service in November upon his request), Frank Köster(starting at the beginning of the year, Luke), Christopf Dahlhaus (starting in May, Mark), Holger, Ricke, Klaus
- **Paul Chang**: Holga(June), Renate
- **Paula Kim**: Christian(Romans), Hans-Hermann Brinkmann, Reiner, Evelin(she has a 17-year-old son)
- **Esther Choe**: Albrecht Swietlick(computer science, 3rd semester. In January-February, he learned Romans), Heidemarie(Genesis. She confessed her oldest sin by studying Romans 3. From February on, she taught Genesis to Brunhilde), Andreas Ganz
- **El**: Günter(electrical science, 10th semester, from September 1984, Mark), Conrad(from July 1984, Mark)
- **Stephan Choe**: Gerd, Ralf, Kersten, Thomas Lehner(Luke 4)
- **Ludger Sickelmann**: Di(Luke), Hans
- **Di**: Thomas, Ralf
- **Karl-Heinz Hohmann**:

- **Rebecca Han**: Monika Würzinger(learned up to Luke Chapter 15 and took a break starting in May), Bernadete Schlonsuk(from Poland, 3rd semester of computer science, Romans starting in March), Waldemar Affa(like Bernadete, lives in the Ostenbergstraße dormitory, 3rd semester of computer science, studying Romans), Martin(learned the 3rd chapter of Mark's Gospel in June and bought the Bible), Tony, Birgit(on Dec. 21)
- **Joseph Han**: Peter Rodenwald, Michael Braam(computer science), Ralf Wortmann(learning Mark starting in July). Michael, Hasso Grope(architect, studying Mark, starting March 9). Francisco(studying Mark and Luke starting in October), Hans-Jürgen Potyka(starting in October), Michael(studying Luke, starting in December)

⋆ God's Work in 1985

In September 1985, Paula Kim moved into a single room at Surck 45 in Dortmund. To save on rent, she prayed to God to share her room with a German student. God answered her prayer immediately, and she was allowed to share her room with **Margarete Jäger**, a Dortmund student. At the time, Margarete was in her third semester of special education and English. She was a Christian with a radiant face and an open heart. Margarete didn't know why she had to go to college, so she considered dropping out of college. She began studying the Bible with Paula Kim and realized that she should study for the glory of God. She also faithfully attended our Sunday worship each week.

At the Thanksgiving Sunday Worship on October 27 of that year, Margarete presented her thoughts on John 1:1-5, saying that Jesus is her light and source of life. Her radiant face reflected her character and faith in Jesus, who gave her great joy.

In December 1985, she began helping other students, such as Irmhild and Kristof, with the Bible study. She also attended the Christmas Conference from December 13 to 15 and gave her testimony, saying that she would learn the Holy Word of God and be saved.

In August 1985, I met **Wolf Tawakol**, a student at the Faculty of Economics at the University of Bochum, and from October I began studying the Bible with him. His father was a doctor from Iran, and his mother was German. Once our family was invited to his house in Dortmund, and his family was very friendly. I realized that this multinational family enriched Germany.

"**Open Bible Evenings**" took place in Dortmund from February 3 to 6 (Sunday-Wednesday).

1st Day

- Preacher: Ralf Nau: "Beginning"(Genesis 1: 1–25)
- Opinion on this Bible text: H-P, Bekkie
- Dance: Y.H. Kornowski

2nd Day

- Preacher: Di: "Meaning of my life"(Genesis 12:1-4)
- Participants: Gisela, Holger, Werner(invited by Esther), Günter, K-H, Di, and El + 9 Koreans

3rd Day

- Preacher: Rebecca Han: "Doubt about God's love"(Genesis 3)
- Solo: Sara
- Flute: K-H
- Participants: Tony, Christoph, Frank, K-H, El, Di + 9 Koreans

4th Day

- Preacher: Karl-Heinz: "Beginning of the new history"(Genesis 12: 1-4)
- Participants: Günter, Holger, Dagmar, Francois, Werner, Di, El, K-H + 9 Koreans

The nationwide **Easter Bible Conference** 1985 took place from May 3 to 5 in the Youth Hotel Rhön.

At **the summer conference** from August 22 to 25(Thursday-Sunday).

Participants: Hans-Peter(Bekkie Lee), Elke(Rebecca Son),

Uwe(El), Gisela(Esther), Wolf(me), Wolfgang & Gabi, Ulrich & Hannenore, Gabi's girlfriend, and her husband were present. (The person in brackets was the one who invited.)

Karl-Heinz gave his testimony: "Jesus made me prince in the kingdom of heaven"(John 1).

We **traveled to Amsterdam** from September 7 to 8(Saturday-Sunday). We camped somewhere near the University of Amsterdam and visited the university, flower gardens, windmills, and more. We were Di, Karl-Heinz, Gabi, Wolfgang, Elke, Hans-Peter, and Korean missionaries.

At a Sunday worship in nature, Wolfgang gave his testimony of faith under the title "The Good Shepherd Knows His Sheep," and Hans-Peter under the title "Jesus Died for My Sins."

I was particularly grateful that God worked through **Ludger** that year. Ludger moved from Cologne to **Krefeld** in the winter semester of 1985/86, where he began studying communications engineering at the College of Applied Sciences. I visited him in his apartment in Krefeld and thanked God that through him God had started the saving work for the students in Krefeld.

My calendar book from December 8, 1985, included the names of the students who had participated one-to-one Bible study with Ludger:

Jürgen Mischke(chemistry 3rd semester) Genesis

Herbert Prinzen(communications engineering, 3rd semester): Genesis 3

Thomas Scholz(communications engineering, 3rd semester) Genesis 2

Lothar Schulz(chemical engineering, 3rd semester) Genesis 1

Horst Dipmann(chemistry, 1st semester): Genesis

⋆ One-to-One Bible Studies 1985

- **Paula Kim**: On March 16, Christian accepted the forgiveness of sins through Mark chapter 2 and attended to the Sunday worship.
  - Margarete - special education, 3rd semester. She learned John's Gospel, Chap. 1 on October 25 and submitted her reflection on it on November 5. She wanted to teach Irmhild the Bible.
  - Kristof learned from Paula on December 15 about John's Gospel and accepted God's grace as a child of God through faith.
  - Evelin learned Genesis from the beginning of the year.
  - Ulrike learned Genesis. Uwe learned the Bible in July and August. Paula prayed that God would use Uwe as a full-time worker for the Lord.
  - Dagmar, Peter(chemical engineering, 1st semester): on November 29, John's Gospel.
- **Di** taught Werner Genesis, lesson 1, and the forgiveness of sins and resurrection on May 7.

- **El** taught Günter, a mechanical engineering student preparing for his diploma thesis, until Mark 16. Chapter. She will start teaching him the Romans. He wanted to attend the Bible conference.
  El also prayed for Uwe.
- **Bekkie Lee**: Mostafa accepted on March 8 the calling through the Gospel of Mark with joy.
  - Hans-Peter learned Mark, Chapter 1. Through the testimony, he confessed Jesus as his Christ and wanted to follow Jesus.
- **Jesaja Lee**: Gabi Großmann(civil engineering), Hartmut Ludwig, Ralf Nau(reported on the traffic accident on August 20), Kristof(Bible study on December 15, he became a child of God through faith on December 20)
- **Rebecca Han**: Tony, Lisa, Holgar, Elke(learned Genesis from June 25). Martin, Monika, Gerd(simply accepted God's word in John 1 on November 6), Francisco
- **Joseph Kim**: Ralf, Hasso, Holger, Andreas, Walter, Dirk, Toni Schönemann(3rd semester, he learned from October 31), Peter Kaltei(in December, John's Gospel), Andreas Uwe(chemical engineering 1st semester), Gerd Bruns
- **Karl-Heinz**: Dirk(for participating in the summer conference), Benedikt, Michael
- **Sara Chang**: K-H, Frank(Genesis, August), Michael Heinke, Peter Kornowski
- **Paul Chang**: Martin, Renate, Markus, Heidrich

- **Esther Choe**: Wolfgang + Gaby Loebert, Petra(participated in the conference at YMCA, Bible study on October 31).
  Esther prayed that El and Gabi would teach others the Bible well.
  On September 15, Gaby preached practical faith in the resurrection based on John 11:23-26.
- **Stephan Choe**: Thomas, Wolfgang, Michael, Ingelore, Norbert, Martin Nachtrodt
  - Wolf Tawakol began studying the Bible on August 5, 1985.
  - Reiner, Heike K.

⋆ **New Year's Symposium 1986**

At the beginning of the New Year, on January 1, 1986, our mission workers shared the 1985 themes of thanksgiving and their 1986 themes of prayer.

Gabi and Wolfgang from Witten were also there. Based on 2 Timothy 2:2, **Gabi** said that she would pray to become a good sheep of God, a good Bible teacher, and be spiritually strong.

Wolfgang said that because of John 12:26, he wanted to follow Jesus, trust God, and use the words of Jesus to feed his sheep.

On that day, we prayed with all our hearts that God would raise hopeful students and young people to be shepherds of His sheep.

Possible shepherd candidates at the time were:

Hans-Peter(chemical engineering 7th semester, 25 years),
Margarete Jäger(special education and German, 3rd sem., 21 years),
Elke(economy 5th semester, 22 years),
Christoph(electrical engineering, 7th semester, 22 years),
Wolf Ebert(business administration, 5th semester, 22 years),
Gaby Bruns(statistics, 3rd semester, 22 years),
Peter Kaltei(chemical engineering, 1st semester)

⋆ Viola Kullmann(since July 1986)

On July 7, 1986, Bekkie Lee reported that a student named Viola Kuhlmann from Hagen enjoyed the Word of God when she studied John 1:1-14 with her. A week later, Viola experienced great joy through studying John 1:19-52 with Bekkie because she learned that God is the owner of her life and that God desires to use her as preciously as Peter.

During the Fall Bible Conference in September 1988, Viola presented her testimony as follows:

"When I was 12, I went to a church children's group for the first time. And I was deeply touched by what Jesus had done for people. During this children's camp, I accepted the Lord Jesus as my Savior. I was really overjoyed that day. I was born again and smiled with joy, knowing that all my sins were forgiven, and my face was beaming. But after about a year, I stopped going to church. I found someone to replace God.

During my studies in Dortmund, missionary Bekkie invited me to the Bible study in May/June 1986. At the 'kind but persistent' invitation of M. Bekkie, I began to study the Bible with M. Bekkie, and I felt great joy in the love of God through the blood of Jesus. I felt my God say to me, 'I love you too.'"

With God's help, Viola passed the state examination as a teacher and also internal exams.

⋆ **Bible Friends 1986:**

- **Paula Kim**: Margarete(until April 1986). Michael Jochmann(student in Bochum, from January 1986). Christof(from January; Paula prayed he would become a shepherd). Renate Buchholz(from mid-December; she was looking for the certainty of her salvation).
- **Joseph Kim**: Peter(from May), Wilson Jameia(from Peru, from May). David Macharia(from Kenya, from November). Braun Surrendra(from July)
- **Bekkie Lee**: H-P Fick(he accepted God's calling based on Mark 12). Mustafa, Eva Mol. Martin(July 14). Viola Kuhlmann(experienced great joy on July 7 through John 1:1 + 14 and accepted Jesus as her person of worship on December 29).
- **Jesaja Lee**: Hartmut Rose(November 15, 1986), Sylvia Hanslik(Special Education 2nd semester, from August). Georg Zurek(College of Applied Sciences for mechanical engineering 4th semester, from June 16, he participated in the summer conference). Nobert(from July 7)

- **Rebecca Han**: Elke(Bible study, since February). Gerd Bruns(statistics 4th semester. In August, he bought a Bible for Bible study and learned to pray in the name of Jesus). Janet Eales(February 4), Christoph(May). Kerstin(elementary school teacher, from June 16). Zita Albrecht(from June 20)
- **Joseph Han**: Gerd Bruns(statistics 4th semester; July 29), Peter Kalteier(from February 4, John's Gospel), Ditmar(John's Gospel), Tony, Walter Histinghaw(chemical engineering 4th semester, from June 23; experienced joy through John 1:5), Francisco Fernandez(June 23), Ludi(June), Malte Lerch(city planning; learned Mark)
- **El:** Günter
- **Di**: Werner(June 2)
- **Esther Choe**: El(Genesis), Gabi(John; Gabi prayed for Hildegart). Petra(April 30). Michaela Kampf(high school student, learned from May). Christiane Koeffler(medicine 2nd semester; wanted to go to thesummer conference, accepted Jesus as God's Lamb in July.)
- **Stephan Choe**: Di(Genesis). Wolf Tawakol(Bochum student, business administration 4th semester). Wolfgang(John 15). Peter Redler. Delef Hüller(June)
- **Sara Chang**: Jürgen Pilhoff. Xian Zhao. Xian Yun(John; understood God's word and simply accepted Jesus. She prayed for Zhao as the shepherd of the Chinese)(September 17, 1986).
- **Paul Chang**: Huan Zhao

* Bible Friends 1987

- **Rebecca Han**: Malte, Zita Albrecht(music), Gerd, Michael, Angela Drellmann, Elke Uhling, Vera Markewitz(in August, John), Margarete Hentschel(in August 7th lesson and found joy)
- **Joseph Han**: Holger Fellensick(mathematics, 3rd semester, learned the 7th step of faith in April), Ulrich(May 5), Bettina, Malte, Michael(music, August)
- **Sara Chang**: Bertram Weiland(arch. 6th semester, learned 7 Steps of Faith and 15th chapter of 1. Corinthians on April 20): Huanly Zhao, Xianyun Zhao(mechanical engineering, learned 1. Corinthians 15: 1-11 on April 17 and wanted to be a witness of the resurrection), Uwe(June 10), Christiane, Margarete Jäger
- **Paul Chang**: Joshi Irischi
- **Bekkie Lee**: H-P Fick learned Genesis and Romans. He learned about rebirth, Jacob's struggle and growth in faith, Viola(Genesis), Eva Moll(IT 11th semester, John), Thomas(March 24), Gibette(English student, Romans 8:28), Hartmut Rose
- **Jesaja Lee**: Norbert, Georg Zurek, Ute, Andreas Bogdan(10th grade high school student, 17 years old, learned 1 Corinthians 15), Udo(7 steps)
- **Di**: Werner(Di prayed for Werner's rebirth, John), Velael(from Egypt), Petra(July 10)
- **El**: Günter(Günter prayed for a job in Dortmund), Udo(January 23, 4th lesson of John), Wellmann(computer science, 7th semester), Bella(taught the 2nd step on June 5 and attended the Sunday worship on July 23)

- **Paula Kim**: Renate(accepted John 1:42. She learned John 11 on April 27 and decided to be a blessing to the medical faculty and prayed to teach Anja Nagel the Bible.)
  Michael Jochmann, Jürgen(participation in the Sunday worship), Markus Grab(participation in the Sunday worship)
- **Joseph Kim**: Tony, Peter, Andreas(one-to-one Genesis Bible study), Joachim(philosophy), Holger(on April 20, 3rd step of 7 steps), Uli(April 27), Michael Neumann, Klaudia(French), Sia(Sunday worship), Solberic, Kita, Wolfgang(medicine, 2nd semester, July 10), Sia(4th step, July 23), Khaij, Tjwan(July 27)
- **Renate Buchholz**: Anja Nagel(Renate's medical colleague). Renate taught Detlef on February 10.
- **Stephan Choe**: Almut Hemmert(law internship after graduation, July 27), Wolf Tawakol, Michael Neumann, Peter Tisch, Klaus Peiler, Seja, Thomas
- **Esther Choe**: Michaela Huber(Sunday worship), Gunda(14th semester)

4. My Mission Report during the Korea Trip in 1986

From October 8 to November 19, 1986, I flew to Korea for a mission report tour. I reported to the student churches in Daejeon; Jongno, Yeonhui, Anam, and Hanyang in Seoul; Daegu; Pohang; Jeonju; Kwangju; Suwon; Chuncheon; Busan; Jeju; Gongju; and Kwanak. During this tour, I received application letters from prospective missionaries. About 70 individuals then submitted their applications to me and expressed their desire to come to Germany as student missionaries.

Around 1988 student churches in Korea were booming, so every student church was overcrowded with students. God sent many student missionaries from these churches into the world. As a result, from 1988 onward, more than 10 student missionaries came to Bochum, and many more also arrived in other cities in Germany, such as Cologne and Dortmund. Thus, most of the German missionaries came as student missionaries.

Eleventh Story: Our Family in Bochum

"For I will pour water on the thirsty land, and streams on the dry ground; I will pour out my Spirit on your offspring, and my blessing on your descendants."
(Isaiah 44:3)

1. Our New Life in Bochum

* Our New Life in Bochum and Esther's Change of Hospital

The first photo: Our first House Church in Bochum: Auf dem Aspei 57, 2nd floor

(from February 28, 1987, to December 31, 1998). The left photo was taken from the entrance side and the right photo from the back of the building. Our House Church was the second apartment from the bottom, with a balcony above the right car.

On November 25, 1986, our family began to pray for a new student church in Bochum and for our move to Bochum. When I decided to move to Bochum, we informed the landlord of our apartment in Dortmund in written form that we would vacate the apartment in Dortmund on February 28, 1987, even though we had not yet found a new apartment in Bochum. I didn't want to delay the move with this termination. If we could not find and move into a new apartment in Bochum by February 28th, our family would have to spend the night on the street. However, since the gracious God provided us with a quiet and cozy apartment at Aspei 57 in Bochum, which was about 700 m east of Bochum University, we moved on February 28. All other units in the building were condominiums. It was an apartment of 86 m^2 with a living room, a bedroom, two small rooms, a kitchen, and a bathroom.

In June of the same year, the Joseph and Paula Kim family moved to Bochum to work with my family. Until September 1987 I preached both for the Sunday worships in Dortmund and the one in Bochum (from May), first at 2 p.m. in Bochum and then at 5 p.m. in Dortmund. Jesaja Lee then took over the leadership and preaching office for the ministry in Dortmund.

A year later, Thomas Hwang and Sarah Oh came from Daejeon in March 1988; each of them lived in a small room in our apartment for a year. Ludger Sickelmann had also lived in a small room in our apartment since mid-1990. He married Grace in late 1990, and the couple stayed in the room for a short time.

Although my family moved to Bochum, Esther had to drive to Dortmund-Hörde for another three years to work the night shift there. Stephan Jr., my first son, attended the "Forest School," the elementary school in front of the Unicenter. Often, I stayed outside with the three-year-old Timothée while Esther slept after her night shift. In June of that year, I took him to a strawberry field and picked strawberries. In this way, I tried not to disturb Esther while she was sleeping after her night shift work.

Timothée on the Strawberry Field in June 1987

I have already told you that I had turned down the offer of a professorship at Chungbuk University(충북 대학교) in Korea. But here in Germany, especially near Bochum, I couldn't find a job with my doctoral degree. About a year later, after moving, I attended a one-year computer course as a software developer in Essen. School fees were paid by the employment office of city Bochum.

Stephan, our older son, switched from elementary school in Dortmund to the second grade of the Forest School in front of Bochum University. He got along well with his classmates, and the teachers liked him. Timothée, our second son, was four years younger than Stephan. Timothée had to stay at home with me or with Mom after we moved to Bochum. When I went to the computer school in Essen, Esther couldn't sleep well after her night shift in the hospital because of him.

Later, Timothée got a place in the Evangelical Kindergarten at "Auf dem Backenberg 6," near our apartment. But he didn't want to go to kindergarten; he was just waiting for his brother to come back from school and play with him. If someone asked him, "Who is your friend?" he replied, "My brother." Stephan loved his brother. With the permission of his teacher and classmates, he took him to school events and proudly introduced him to his classmates and teacher.

After completing the computer course, I sent numerous applications to companies but couldn't find a job. Then I realized God's will and decided to work as a full-time preacher and serve in the student Bible study ministry. In these circumstances, God led me to devote myself fully to missionary work.

*** Esther's Wise and Devoted Help**

After our family moved from Dortmund to Bochum at the end

of February 1987, Esther couldn't quickly find a job in Bochum. So she commuted by car to the Evangelical Hospital Bethanien in Dortmund-Hörde. After three years, by God's grace, she found employment at the Bethanien Hospital near Bochum Central Station and worked there in the departments of internal medicine and of ear, nose, and throat medicine since September 1991. She had hoped that after I received my doctorate, I would get a job and take care of the family's financial needs. But she never complained to me, even though I had decided to work full-time for the student ministry without income.

After a while, our student church paid me a small amount each month. Esther worked about 70% of a full-time job as a nurse's aide. Therefore, her wages were not enough for the family if she had not used them sparingly. But she managed the household so frugally with her very limited income. In order to handle family finances economically, she studied the market's weekly specials and bought the necessary food and household goods. Although she was thrifty, she gave generously to others and served God's work with her heart. At the hospital where she worked, I had two or three operations for a middle ear infection. Esther was weak and tired after work, but she still looked after me. I am deeply grateful to my wife for her help and dedication.

On July 31, 2009, when she was legally 60 years old, she retired five years before the mandatory retirement age. She didn't want me to worry about our finances. So, she took responsibility for the household and created a bank account in her name. But she always kept enough money in one place so

I could use it as needed. When she was diagnosed with cancer, she made her bank account a joint account for both of us. Esther rarely bought new clothes but always dressed beautifully and elegantly. She taught our sons that too. She always kept the apartment clean and tidy.

2. Visiting Korea in 2002 and Carrying Out an "Impossible Mission"

Before I traveled to Korea in January 2002, Esther asked me to lead her older sister to faith in Jesus. She told me to make this impossible mission "possible" and save her sister. When I arrived in Jangheung by express bus, Esther's sister-in-law picked me up and took me by taxi to Esther's sister's house. I stayed there one night, pondering how I could fulfill this "impossible mission" and encourage Esther's sister to believe in Jesus Christ. Then I decided to thank her for her kindness. Esther's sister had served me the best dishes, such as expensive and delicious fish, shrimp, mussels, and salads. That made me feel her love for Esther. We talked a lot. The next day, before I left, I told her that Esther had asked me to invite her to believe in Jesus Christ. Esther's sister replied, "I cannot guarantee that I will believe." Her response showed that she wanted to believe in Jesus. I was very grateful to God for that. In a way, I accomplished the "impossible" mission. I prayed that God would help her believe.

It was January 8, 2002, when we returned to Daejeon from Jangheung. That's when I heard the news that Missionary Samuel C. Lee in Chicago, the General Secretary of UBF Worldwide, had suffocated to death from smoke in his bathroom. The pastors and leaders of the UBF reformers flew to Chicago to attend his funeral.

On January 11, I drove from Daejeon to Seoul to meet Pastor David Lim. When I was a sophomore and he was a freshman, he had studied the Bible with me. He then took over the Student Friday Bible Group from me. That's why he was a very important person to me. Today, he is the pastor of three churches in and around Seoul, with a total of nearly 10,000 attendees. Pastor Lim adapted the discipleship method he had learned in our student church to the circumstances of his church and encouraged his churchgoers to become disciples of Jesus. He continued to pray sincerely for the world mission. I thanked God for blessing Pastor David's prayer and devotion.

3. Stephan's and Timothée's Degrees and Their Jobs

I grew up in a poor family and suffered from an injured hip. To survive, I had to study hard and always be the best student in school and university to get a scholarship. This led me to believe that my opinion was always the best. Because of my self-centered mindset, it took me many years to listen to other people's opinions and recognize their wisdom. So I prayed that my sons would get good grades, but not the best grades among their classmates, so that my sons could appreciate and understand others well. God answered my prayers.

From September 1985, Stephan attended the "Ostenberg Elementary School" next to the Margaretenkapelle in Dortmund. After moving to Bochum, Stephan attended the "Forest School" in front of the University of Bochum from March 1987 to spring 1989. He then attended the "Einstein Gymnasium"(the German school form of middle and high school) near the city center. In Germany, the gymnasium lasted nine years after completing the four years of elementary school. Gymnasiums in Germany are primarily intended to prepare for university studies and currently have an eight-year system in many federal states. Students at the university completed their studies with a diploma. The university diploma was roughly equivalent to the bachelor's and master's degrees in Korea. The diploma course could be completed in approximately five years, but on average, it took six and a half years.

The first year of university study in Korea offered general education subjects such as cultural history, English, Korean, and philosophy, etc. From the second year onward, students primarily studied their specialized subjects. In Germany, however, students already learn these general subjects at the upper level of gymnasium.

When Stephan and Timothée graduated from gymnasium with their diplomas, military service was still an obligation for boys over eighteen years with German citizenship. Instead of military service, Stephan worked for about a year as a paramedic for the "Samaritan Association," transporting emergency patients to hospitals by ambulance. Through this work, Stephan acquired extensive medical knowledge and wanted to study medicine after his service.

Then Esther said to him, "If you have a clear calling as a doctor, you can study medicine. But if you want to become a doctor to earn money, you'd better not study medicine."

In October 1999, Stephan began studying economics at the University of Bochum.

Our second apartment in Bochum, Gropiusweg 11 (Right side of the 3rd floor; January 1, 1999 - March 31, 2010) and our third apartment (Left side of the 5th floor; from April 1, 2010, to today)

At other universities in Germany, one had to choose a minor if you were studying economics or business administration. But at the University of Bochum, they studied economics and business administration together without a minor.

After completing his degree in economics in May 2004, Stephan started working at Ernst & Young in Düsseldorf and conducted financial audits for many companies. Thus, Stephan had to travel a lot by car. Stephan is someone who remains loyal to one company. Therefore, after moving to Chicago, USA, he continued to work for this company. When we gave up our Korean citizenship and took German citizenship to serve the evangelization of Germans, we also changed the citizenship of our two sons to German citizenship.

Timothée also entered the primary school "Waldschule" in Bochum in 1990 and attended it for four years. He then attended the "Einstein Gymnasium" for nine years and completed his studies with good grades. Before graduating from gymnasium, Timothée completed a one- or two-month internship at the branch of the city library in the Unicenter and organized the books on the shelves. From the discarded books, he brought me ten volumes of "Handbook of Church History"(Herder Publisher). For the 10th anniversary of our student church in Bochum, our coworkers made a small brochure from this book entitled "The Persecution of the First Christians."

After graduating from the gymnasium, Timothée worked as a helper for the disabled at the Sumperkamp 9-15 student residence in the University Center from fall 2003 to 2004, rather than serving in the military for about a year.

After studying economics at the University of Bochum for around nine semesters, starting in October 2004, he received a good certificate as a Diploma-Volkswirt at the graduation ceremony in the university's Audimax on May 18, 2009.

Stephan has many friends and continues to maintain his relationships with them. He resembles me in many ways; he studied hard and worked diligently with perseverance.

Timothée is very similar to Esther; he is creative and has a fine sensibility. He's also the type to concentrate; he almost never slept and focused on preparing when an exam was approached.

We couldn't take optimal care of our children because Esther worked, I pursued my doctorate, and we both gave Bible lessons to students in the evenings. So, I could understand why Stephan asked me the following questions. When Stephan was in gymnasium, he once asked me, "Why do you love the coworkers of the church more than us, your children?"

I replied, "I love you more than the coworkers of the church. But I try to love the coworkers of the church as I love you."

After hearing this answer, Stephan stopped asking this question.

How did both of them finance their university tuition fees? In Germany, students–except for some private universities–do not have to pay tuition fees because the state covers all university costs. Instead, students need money for their living expenses.

You also have the opportunity to apply to the state for a 'BAföG' for around four years. You can repay this money within a few years of graduation. Both sons received BaföG. They also worked part-time, for example, at Kentucky Fried Chicken or in the cinema in Bochum-Langendreer.

After completing his studies, our second son, Timothée, worked for a year in a Korean-run company in Bochum. The company didn't adhere to working hours and let him work until the evening. So, Timothée changed firms and worked at a firm in Essen similar to his brother's firm. He then moved to the Werhahn KG headquarters in Neuss as an accountant. The company is a large international firm with around 10,000 employees. The Twin Knife Company is also a subsidiary of this company.

4. Stephan's Marriage

Left: Wedding photo at the registry office in Bochum-Gerthe in December 2008

Right: Wedding photo with parents in the church in Seoul in March 2009. We stood on the left and Seungmi's parents on the right.

After graduating from university, Stephan lived in Düsseldorf and attended the Full Gospel Church there, where he met a Korean student, Seungmi Lee. In Germany, the civil wedding usually takes place first at the city hall and then the church wedding. First, Stephan married her in December 2008 at the city hall in Bochum-Gerthe. At this wedding, an official explained the laws of marriage to the newlyweds in front of two witnesses(Esther and Timothée). The bride and groom then signed the marriage certificate. The officer then announced that the two had become a married couple and gave a congratulatory speech.

We thought about a church wedding in Germany, but it wouldn't be easy for Seungmi's family members and relatives in Korea to come to Germany and attend the wedding. So I suggested to Stephan that we hold the church wedding in Korea. Stephan and Seungmi flew to Korea on February 28, and Esther and I flew there on March 3 and back on March 28. Timothée also arrived, and many of Stephan's friends came from Germany for the wedding.

Two or three days before that wedding, the bride's family invited us to an introductory meeting of the bride and groom's families. When we got married, there was no such custom, so Esther and I didn't know anything about this tradition. We thought the bride's parents just wanted to get to know us. So we put on comfortable clothes and went to the meeting point. When my older brother saw that we were leaving, he said to us: "Do you want to go there like that?" and said no more. When we arrived at the meeting place, lo! The bride's whole family had dressed up! The bride's parents told us that they were nervous at first but calmed down when they saw us in our everyday clothes.

The church wedding of Stephan and Seungmi was held on a Saturday in March 2009 at 1:00 PM at the Flower Garden Church in Nowon-gu, Seoul, where Jong-Jun Kim(김종준) was the pastor. My siblings and relatives, Esther's siblings and relatives, and Seungmi's parents, siblings, and relatives attended this wedding. About ten former fellow students of mine and many friends of Stephan and Seungmi participated.

Pastor Jong-Jun Kim said his congratulations and encouragement were based on the Word of Ephesians 5:22-25:

> "Wives, submit yourselves to your own husbands as you do to the Lord. For the husband is the head of the wife as Christ is the head of the church, his body, of which he is the Savior. Now as the church submits to Christ, so also wives should submit to their husbands in everything.
>
> Husbands, love your wives, just as Christ loved the church and gave himself up for her."

After this church wedding, "Pyebaek"(폐백) took place, at which the newly married couple expressed their respect and gratitude to the parents of both sides according to the Korean tradition.

We then took a bus to a hostel with three large rooms. There, the bride and groom celebrated all night with their friends. Seungmi's parents, Esther, and I stayed in the room next to their party room. I could hardly sleep because of their celebration.

On Sunday morning, around 4 AM, the bus arrived and

took us to the Flower Garden Church. After the early morning worship, we had breakfast with Seungmi's parents. Afterwards, the bride and groom drove to the airport to fly back to Germany, because Stephan had to return to work.

On Sunday morning, Esther and I visited Mi-Ri Park(박미리), a daughter of Esther's sister in Nowon-gu(노원구), Seoul. In the evening, we briefly visited my brother and then stayed overnight with my third sister.

The next day, Esther visited her nieces in Seoul and then drove to Jangheung to visit her sister. I stayed with my brother for a few days. When I heard that Young-Seon Cho(조영선), the son of Hyun-Sook Choe(최현숙), my brother's first daughter, had fallen down the stairs and broken his leg, and was in Gil Hospital(길병원) in Incheon, I visited him and then went to see Pastor David Woo in Incheon.

On the Wednesday evening, March 15, David Woo drove me to the "Jesusfull Church"(충만한 교회) in Ilsan(일산), where David Lim serves as pastor. Ilsan is a satellite city of Seoul.

Pastor Lim invited me to share my experiences of faith in Jesus and my ministry in Germany at his church.

The next day, I took an express bus to Jangheung(장흥), Esther's hometown, and reunited with her at her sister's house. On Saturday, we went to my mother church in Daejeon. The next day, we attended Sunday worship. Afterward, we briefly visited my third sister in Seoul before returning to Germany.

5. Stephan's Family Flies to the USA

After the wedding, Stephan and our daughter-in-law moved to Heidelberg for her study of music therapy at a private university in Heidelberg. In early October 2010, their first child, Sophia Erin, was born. Stephan and Marie Seungmi were overjoyed and decorated their living room with festive decorations on the 100th day after the birth and also on her first birthday.

Shortly before the birth, Marie's mother arrived from Korea and looked after Marie and the baby for about a month. Afterward, Esther took care of the baby. She took the train to Heidelberg and cared for the baby while Marie was at college. Esther came to Bochum on weekends and returned to Heidelberg on Mondays. Esther was very happy to look after her granddaughter. Esther said she wanted to live until Sophia got married. Marie tried to make Esther and me happy. She often visited us and cooked for us.

In August 2013, Stephan's family flew to Chicago because Stephan had started a new job at his company there. His family lived in Evanston, near Chicago. The second grandchild, Sean Isu, was born in early October. Marie's mother came from Korea and cared for Marie and her baby for about a month. Esther, Timothée, and I visited the family on November 16 and stayed for two weeks. We took a photo with Lake Michigan in the background.

Marie taught both children piano, and Stephan and Marie took Sophia to figure skating and Sean to hockey. Both helped the children find faith in Jesus.

Family photo taken on the shores of Lake Michigan in November 2013

I had been to the United States several times to attend the Summer Bible Conference, but I had not seen the reality of the United States. This visit gave me a glimpse into the reality of the USA. Stephan guided us through the city center and took us on a boat ride. We also climbed Chicago's tallest building and looked out over the city.

Parking in downtown Chicago costs about $16 an hour, and I saw people begging in front of the skyscraper. While cars stopped briefly at a red light, poor people came out onto the lane and begged the drivers for money. This showed that the U.S. is a society with a huge gap between the rich and the poor.

On Sunday, we visited an American church that our son and daughter-in-law attended and met missionary Grace Park. She had graduated from the Art School of Seoul National University and attended Jongno Student Church in Seoul, Korea. She had taught Bekkie Lee the Bible. Grace Park invited Esther and me to her home. I learned that this family had suffered greatly from poverty and a car accident. They are like a dying grain of wheat on earth for the hope of Jesus in the mission field. I believed and prayed that God would richly bless this family.

6. Our 70th Birthday

I have already stated that Esther and I share a birthday. On our birthday in July 2018, I told Andreas, Renate, and Esther that after exactly one year, I would hand over the preaching and leadership of the church to Andreas. And I asked them not to make this public. Of course, I didn't know at that time that Esther would get cancer.

The day before Esther's and my birthdays in 2019, Stephan's entire family from Evanston, USA, and Timothée visited us. The next day, Sunday, we were going to celebrate our 70th birthday. On that 70th birthday, I had planned to hand over the preaching office and leadership of our church to Andreas Schmeinck. However, we received a call from Korea informing us that my brother had passed away and would be buried two days later, on Monday. I was hesitant to fly to Korea because of the handover of the ministry. But Esther advised me to fly to Korea immediately to attend my brother's funeral. Timothée quickly bought a plane ticket for that day, and I flew to Korea that evening.

My brother was buried right next to my parents near our childhood home. The day after the funeral, I went once more to his grave with my brother's daughters and his son and planted grass on the grave. Then I returned to Germany the following Friday, preached my last sermon on Sunday, and handed over the preaching and leadership position to Andreas. Thus, the handover of leadership was accomplished at the right time, just as God had planned. God's plan is perfect. I give all the glory to God. That day, the church prepared cakes for my 70th and Esther's 71st birthdays. We thanked God for our lives.

Our birthday party in 2019 at the church

Twelfth Story: We Share Good News with the Students in Bochum

"The Spirit of the Lord is on me, because he has anointed me to proclaim good news to the poor. He has sent me to proclaim freedom for the prisoners and recovery of sight for the blind, to set the oppressed free, to proclaim the year of the Lord's favor." (Luke 4:18-19)

"He told them, 'The harvest is plentiful, but the workers are few. Ask the Lord of the harvest, therefore, to send out workers into his harvest field.'" (Luke 10:2)

1. Beginning of Our Student Church in Bochum

Since 1978, our coworkers had invited students from Bochum, Essen, and Dortmund to Bible studies and Sunday worship at the Bible House in Dortmund. However, it was difficult for students from Essen or Bochum to attend church worship in Dortmund. Therefore, some coworkers from Essen and Bochum moved to Dortmund in order to concentrate on the student ministry there. Renate Buchholz, a medical student in her first semester at the University of Bochum, began to study the Bible with Paula Kim in December 1986 and to attend our Sunday worship. Her visit was like a signal from God that we should become active in the student mission in Bochum. That was why our family and Paula and Joseph Kim's family moved to Bochum.

On February 28, 1987, our family first moved from Dortmund to Bochum, Auf dem Aspei 57, about 700 meters east of the University of Bochum. In July of the same year, the family of Joseph and Paula Kim moved to Bochum. Starting on May 24, we held Sunday worship at 2:00 p.m. in our rented apartment in Bochum. After this worship, I drove to Dortmund and preached there at 5:00 p.m. I preached twice more until September 20 of that year. The Dortmund church was located in a first-floor apartment of the Hannibal Tower Building (Vogelpothsweg 16-18). On September 27, Jesaja Lee began preaching on Sundays as the new leader of the Dortmund church. On October 18 of the same year, the Dedication Worship of the new church building took place.

2. Story of the German Student Co-workers

*** Renate Buchholz (married Schmeinck) & Andreas Schmeinck**

Renate grew up in a believing family because her father was a pastor in a Protestant church. However, she had no firm conviction that she was saved. In October 1986, she began her medical studies at the University of Bochum. In mid-December of that year, she met Paula Kim at the university and told her about the uncertainty of her salvation. Paula then told her that God could give her the conviction of her salvation through His Word. After attending the Christmas conference, Renate began studying the Bible with Paula Kim and worked with us in student ministry.

Thus, she became one of the co-workers of our Bochum student church. She spoke kindly to students, helped them trust in our church, and taught them the Bible. Starting in 1989, Renate, Pauline Lee, and Esther Bae lived together for some time in an apartment in the Unicenter across the street from the university. This helped them to understand each other well across nationalities and cultures and to work with one heart in the student mission. Renate helped medical students such as Anja Willkommen, Ulrike Brinkmann, Christa, and Stephanie with their Bible studies. Nevertheless, she did not neglect her studies and successfully passed the final examination in June 1993. On June 13, 1993, there was a Thanksgiving Sunday worship for her graduation from the university, and she presented her testimony of faith. Part of her testimony was as follows:

"As a daughter of a pastor in a Christian home, I learned my personal belief in God and Jesus from childhood. However, as I grew older, I began to doubt my Christian-being because there had been no clear conversion experience in my life and I couldn't say anything about my rebirth or certainty of salvation. I wanted to be a Christian and live according to God's standards, but in my heart, like unbelievers, I compromised with sin. I wanted to live for God, but since I didn't know a holy life, I was desperate and had no inner certainty about my salvation. At that time, I often wept at night and asked God to show me what I still lacked. In this desperate situation, I remembered a Bible verse that touched me so deeply that I had copied it and had hung it in my mirror. It was Deuteronomy 1:21, 'See, the LORD your God has given you the land. Go up and take possession of it as the LORD, the God of your ancestors, told you. Do not be afraid; do not be discouraged.'

This verse had given me hope that God had something else in store for me. God saw me very well and guided me with His goodness. He gave me a place to study medicine in Bochum. During my first semester, Missionary Paula Kim invited me to the Christmas conference. Because she told me convincingly that God's Word could certainly solve my inner problems, I gained confidence and the feeling that God had sent her to me. After the conference, I began the Bible study with her. One of my problems was that I didn't take God at His Word. But Paula and Stephan encouraged me again and again to believe in God's Word. For example, God promised me in John 1:12, 'Yet to all who did receive him, to those who believed in his name, he gave the right to become children of God.' But for a long time, I couldn't overcome my doubts about my salvation because I thought I would have to look different if I were already safely saved.

Finally, God helped through Romans 1:17, which says, 'For in the gospel the righteousness of God is revealed—a righteousness that is by faith from first to last, just as it is written: 'The righteous will live by faith.' I realized that faith in Jesus alone makes me righteous before God, and that I must always hold on to that faith, no matter how weak or inadequate I am. I decided to stop allowing doubts and to simply hold on to the belief that Jesus had already done everything necessary for me. Then I could enjoy my salvation. I learned that I had to fight the doubts that kept arising afterward and to hold on to God's Word, which is reliable.

Second, through His Word, God helped me recognize myself as a lost sinner and acknowledge the filthiness of my heart's desires before God's holiness. I learned that God wants everyone to love Him, their Creator, with a pure heart and worship Him alone as their God. From then on, I wanted to live a pure life and worship only Jesus as my Savior and true man. God trained me not only to recognize my weakness and sinfulness, but also to purify my heart and live a sanctified life by repenting and accepting the Jesus' death for my sins. Through this struggle, God helped me to be convinced of my salvation and my belonging to Him.

God not only wanted to save me from sin, but also had a great plan for me. At a conference during my first semester break, I was particularly interested in the Word in Genesis 12:1+2, through which God called Abraham, <The LORD had said to Abram, 'Go from your country, your people and your father's household to the land I will show you. I will make you into a great nation, and I will bless you; I will make your name great, and you will be a blessing.'>

I realized that God had high hopes in an old, flawed man to make him a great nation and blessing to the world, and that God kept his promise 100 percent when Abraham kept God's Word. I chose this word as the word of the year and later also as my life motto because I so desired to be a blessing to many. I accepted it as a calling and God's new country for me that God wanted to make me a blessing, especially among the students in Germany and beyond, all over the whole world, and thanked God for the great hope He placed in me. God blessed my small decision by appointing me as a shepherdess of students at the Ruhr University and repeatedly entrusting me with students at the medical faculty for 1:1 Bible studies. After most of them broke off their Bible studies when it was time to take a concrete step of faith or repent, God led Anja Willkommen, also a medical student, to a one-to-one Bible study. In her search for God, she had attended various church events, but through studying the Bible, she was able to find clear answers and meet Jesus as her personal Savior. Because of the love of Jesus, who freed her from her inner darkness, fear and searching, she decided, based on John 12:24 to dedicate her life to the salvation of the students.

Six months later, God led my fellow student Ulrike Brinkmann to Bible study. Her mother had prayed for her a lot.

...

She realized through God's Word that only a life with God, her Creator, has absolute meaning and decided to entrust her life completely to God. I started studying the Bible in my first semester.

...

After lectures at the University, I often had to rush to get to Bible study on time. But God has always shown that He keeps His promise in Matthew 6:33 and provides for all our needs if we seek first His kingdom. I often dreaded my exams. But during my six and a half years of medical studies, God helped me pass all but one of my minor subjects on the first attempt, so that a fellow student was amazed and said he wanted to become a Christian too.

I praise God's faithfulness and strength, which He has shown me through His grace."

When Andreas was working at the Cologne student church, he hung the invitation posters on the street wall. Eberhard Gross, the current church leader and preacher of the Cologne UBF, saw the posters and came to the church. Andreas also helped Norbert in Cologne and remained loyal to him as his friend and advisor until Norbert, suffering from cancer, went to the Heavenly Father.

Renate and Andreas became engaged in April 1992 and married in September 1993 at the town hall and celebrating their church wedding at the conference center in Rehe. After completing his studies, Andreas worked as a trainee teacher at a private school for two years. He then began working full-time in our church.

This couple continued to play an important role in the student ministry of our church in Bochum. Andreas is a faithful servant of the Lord and helped many students in Bochum with the Bible study, including Jörg, Christoph, Oriel, and others.

On July 21, 2019, he took over from me as preacher and church director and faithfully serves the church through preaching and prayer.

David, the first child of Andreas and Renate, completed a master's degree in mechanical engineering at the University of Bochum. He is an important contributor to our church's work. Mariela, the couple's second child, is also an indispensable and significant member of our church.

⋆ Hartmut Rose

Paula and Jesaja had already visited him in the summer of 1983(the first semester of electrical engineering). After that, Jesaja and Bekkie Lee invited him to a Bible study. However, due to the distance, we couldn't really help him well with the Bible study. When we began our work in Bochum, we invited him to Sunday worship and to Bible studies, and he enjoyed coming. He worked with us warmly. He graduated from the university with good honors in 1990 and worked as a research assistant at the university.

The second Student Church in Bochum: Hustadtring 143
(The apartment on the 3rd floor with a satellite receiver on the balcony)

⋆ Anja Willkommen (married Wilms)

Anja came to our church in her first year of study at the Medical Faculty of the University of Bochum. Starting in 1989, she studied the Bible with Sarah Oh, Renate, and Paula Kim; learned about Jesus personally; and served the Lord faithfully in the church. But she didn't neglect her medical studies. After graduating, she married Guido Wilms in Aachen and moved to Aachen, where she also faithfully serves God.

⋆ Ludger Sickelmann

Ludger had worked with us devotedly in Dortmund. In the meantime, he had moved to Cologne and then to Krefeld. On June 30, 1990, he moved from Krefeld to Bochum and worked with us in Bochum for the student mission. At the end of 1990, he married Grace. By the end of November 1991, he successfully completed his training as a computer specialist.

Grace Sickelmann came to Germany on April 2, 1991. She gave birth to her first child, Sarah, her second child, Deborah, and her third child, Paulina. The couple raised three daughters well.

Ludger actively invited students to Bible study. In particular, he helped Andreas Lange and Igor from Minsk to live as disciples of Jesus.

In 2002, his family moved to Essen to offer Bible studies to students in Essen. Ludger is now a schoolteacher and Grace is also a teacher for the learning disabled. The couple worked actively for the student mission in a Free Evangelical Church in Essen and helped many students, including Chinese, with the Bible study. They have now started a new home church and are helping young people. The couple is also working to open a Christian school.

⋆ Ulrike Brinkmann (married Gross)

In mid-February 1991, she was invited by Renate to study the Bible. At this point, she was in the 9th semester of her medical studies. She studied the Bible first with Renate and then with Paula Kim. Through God's Word from Genesis 1:31, she received much joy because she realized that God created her well and is very happy with her. Out of joy for God's love, she told her father about God's love. She also received great grace through divine forgiveness and blessings in John chapters 4 and 8:11.

She and Eberhard Gross married in July 1994 in the

conference room in Rehe. The couple has a son named Paul. Ulrike works as an orthopedic surgeon. She also faithfully helps students with the Word of God.

On August 22, 1992, she presented her testimony at the Summer Bible Conference, which states, among other things:

"I was the baby of the family and received a lot of love from my parents. But little by little I became dependent on this human love and affection.

In the spring of 1986, my grandmother suffered a stroke and needed care. This illness made me feel very helpless. My relatives and I watched, more or less helplessly, as she died of another stroke six months later after several weeks in intensive care. I developed a desire to overcome my helplessness and be able to help other people effectively. That's why I began studying medicine at the Ruhr University in Bochum in the fall of 1986. But the studies failed to meet my expectations in any way.

In the clinical semesters, I was confronted more with illness and death and with the fact that even the best doctor cannot prevent everyone from dying at some point. My inner helplessness remained. The question of what meaning my life actually has tormented me. In the winter of 1990/91, I reached my lowest point. Everything I had done so far seemed pointless and superfluous; my studies, fleeting joy, student parties - nothing could really make me happy.

In February 1991, Renate Buchholz asked me if I would be interested in starting a Bible study with her. In my little free time, of all things, I had no real interest in studying the Bible, and I didn't even know Renate very well. However, since it was a winter vacation, I couldn't find an appropriate excuse and was too polite to simply reject this bold proposal.

So, I started the seven-step Bible study with Renate. In the second step,

I was amazed to find that I was created after God. God did not say, 'You were created wrongly,' but, 'You are very good!' This word has made a deep impression on me. Here I could see for the first time that my life is not meaningless, but that God loves me and created me for His glory and according to His plan, and that there is no happy life without a personal relationship with God.

In the summer semester of 1991, I began to learn the Gospel of John from Missionary Paula Kim. Through chapter 4, I recognized my sin of worshiping men. This caused a serious conflict for me. ... I realized that a clear decision was necessary on this point, but I didn't have the strength to do it alone. Through John 8:1-11, I was able to accept the forgiving love of Jesus, who said to me, 'I don't condemn you like that, Ulrike. Go and sin no more.' He did not condemn me, but patiently accepted me with all my shortcomings and weaknesses. He completely forgave me for my sin and gave me a new direction in life to put Him first in my life. I made a clear decision for God.

He has now clearly trained me through the practical year and the completion of my doctoral thesis. Even though the connection between everyday hospital life, my doctoral thesis, and church life often seems impossible to me, I now know that nothing is really impossible with God. I thank Him for freeing me from a useless and meaningless life and giving me a new life orientation to serve Him. I pray that God would use me as His tool to pass on His Word to medical students in Bochum."

⋆ Andreas Lange

In 1993, Ludger invited Andreas Lange, an electrical engineering student, to the Summer Bible Conference, and after the conference, he helped him with the Bible study of seven steps, the Gospel of John, and Genesis. Through this, Andreas came to know Jesus' love for sinners personally. He is generous and kind. He helped Joachim.

Andreas presented his testimony of faith at the Summer Bible Conference. Excerpt from his testimony dated Aug. 19, 1994:

"My old life:

My name is Andreas Lange. I am studying electrical engineering in my 12th semester. My parents raised me Catholic from childhood. But as I grew up, I longed for loud music, soccer games, searching for a girl, parties, and so on. That was the center of my life. But I couldn't find what I was looking for. On the contrary, my daily life became darker and darker. I was filled with hatred and desire. I pretended to change, but I failed.

God worked in me: In my dark situation, God showed me that confessing my moral sins to a priest could help me. I thought this was a good chance for me and repented of all my sins. Shortly afterward, I received an invitation to Bible studies, prayer meetings, and so on. Eventually, in 1993, I attended the Summer Bible Conference and subsequently began my one-to-one Bible study.

God gave me Ludger Sickelmann as my personal Bible teacher. Through this Bible study, I learned the heart and love of Jesus for sinners like me and others. And I recognized the great opportunity for all people to be saved from their sins. I learned the <Seven Steps of Faith>, then the Gospel of John, and now Genesis. My worldly desires gradually disappeared. I thank God for His mighty work in me."

The third Student Church in Bochum: Hustadtring 141, 3rd floor (from April 1, 1994, to 2003.) The apartment with the fourth balcony from below.

⋆ Stefan Schulzki

In the fall of 1994, Samuel Park invited him and Stefan studied God's Word with Peter Bae. This led him to faith in the Gospel and to his participation in our mission work. Later, he married a devout woman in the Lutheran Church and invited the Bae and Schmeinck families, as well as me, to his wedding celebration.

⋆ Stephanie

In early March 1997, Renate Schmeinck invited Stephanie to a Bible study and taught her the Book of Genesis. On July 11, 1997, during a Bible study with Renate, she received the assurance of salvation through the Word of God in John 5:24. From the winter semester of 1998/99 until March 1999, she lived with the Schmeinck family in a shared apartment. In December 1998, she began working actively as a co-worker. In early 1999, she chose Matthew 6:33–34 as her annual guiding verses and testified that God had accepted her faith in Him and helped her prepare for the Physikum(the basic medical examination). She helped her parents with the Bible study.

In early 1998, she had presented her annual key verse symposium on the guiding verse of the year, John 14:1. She said:

"The year 1997 marked a decisive turning point in my life: In that year, I came to know Jesus Christ personally through Bible study. I experienced my rebirth in the summer of 1997 when, while studying the Gospel of John, I realized that I was lost and accepted the salvation offered in Jesus Christ. I would like to explain this in more detail. Until that summer, I was trapped in this world and enslaved by my sins: I was selfish, greedy, envious, skeptical, and unbelieving because I loved recognition, money, and success more than God. I wanted to achieve something better than my parents had done in their lives. I understood that the crucial thing was missing in my life when Jesus said to me in John 4:14, 'But whoever drinks the water I give them will never thirst. Indeed, the water I give them will become in them a spring of water welling up to eternal life.' I realized that I had only satisfied my physical needs, not my spiritual ones. I had completely neglected my relationship with God, and that had made me so unhappy and desperate. I had always longed for more, because the world cannot satisfy our spiritual needs. Only God or His incarnate Son, Jesus, can do this.

By spiritual needs, I mean the following: God created me in His image and gave me His Spirit. Only as a unity of body and spirit did I become a living being. My spirit or soul is like God and finds joy only when I speak with God and acknowledge Him as my Creator and Lord. My thirst for recognition, knowledge, peace, and so on could therefore only be quenched through Jesus. He freed me from my sins and my selfishness, thus taking away my earthly life.

He gave me the living water, His Spirit, to quench my thirst and transform me into His image.

Through His Word in John 5:24, He gave me the hope of eternal life and thus took away my fear of living under the power of death. He answers all of my questions, for He shared with me everything He had heard from the Father, that is, from God (John 15:15).

I also learned that by telling others about Jesus, I myself can become a source of eternal life for others. This is how my mother began to understand that she, too, needed salvation through Jesus. My parents overcame their skepticism and accompanied me to Sunday worship in our church at the end of the year."

⋆ Igor Poleshchuk

After participating in the Moscow Summer Conference in 1992, Igor came to Bochum as an exchange student and stayed in Bochum for seven months. Through Ludger Sickelmann, he studied God's Word and experienced heartfelt love from all coworkers. After returning in 1993 to Minsk, he helped many students and married a woman of faith. Ludger, some coworkers from Bochum, and I traveled to Minsk by train and attended his wedding.

⋆ Yurim Sim

She had regularly attended our Sunday worship since August 9, 2015. She also invited Chan-Il Chung and Eun-Hee Lim and their three daughters, Hye-Young, Ui-Yeong, and Seon-Yeong, as well as Kyo-Eun Koo and her husband, Karl, a little later. Yurim studied the Bible with Renate. After graduating from university, she got a job in Frankfurt in 2024 and moved there.

Photos of the entrance and balcony of the 4th Student Church (2nd floor) at Markstraße 120, Bochum (from March 1, 2004, to the present)

Before this apartment, we used the fellowship room of the student residence at Laerholzstraße 84 as a Sunday worship room for about one year (2003–2004).

3. Story of the Bible Friends in Bochum

⋆ Bible Friends in the Beginning (approx. 1978 – 1992)

Since we began our mission work in Bochum, many students have studied God's Word with us and come to know Jesus Christ. I would like to mention just a few here.

- Christa

Since the beginning of October 1988, Christa has studied the Seven Steps of Faith together with Renate. Through this, she has developed a trusting relationship with Jesus, like that between a small child and his mother.

- Michael Sander

Michael Sander began studying God's Word with Joseph Kim in December 1987, and in 1988, he studied the entire Gospel of John. He was a brilliant mechanical engineering student. We prayed that he would be a great blessing like Abraham, and we believed that God would surely answer our prayer.

- Almut Hemmert

In 1987, I met Almut Hemmert, a law student, in the student residence at Sumperkamp. She was a confessing Christian and led a Bible study group in her home. She passed her state exam that same year. Likewise, she encouraged me to boldly invite the students to participate in the Bible study group.

- Anja Nagel

Anja Nagel was a fellow student of Renate's. At the beginning of their studies, the two lived together in an apartment. One early summer day (it was a weekend or a public holiday at the end of May or beginning of June 1988), our coworkers camped in the fields belonging to Anja's parents in the Sauerland region, as Anja's parents were farmers. Anja now works as a doctor.

- Michael Jochmann

His parents financially supported a Korean schoolgirl through the SOS Children's Village. Therefore, in the fall of 1988, he posted a notice on the bulletin board in the student dormitory on Stiepelerstraße seeking a Korean translator. He was in his eighth semester studying electrical engineering. Then Paula Kim contacted him, and they began studying the Bible together. He was so enthusiastic about God's Word that he studied it regularly with her and wrote down his personal impressions and decisions based on the biblical text. He readily provided his car for the trip to the conference, participated in the Bible conference, and shared his testimony of faith.

Having not truly known God before, he sought the meaning of life in fellowship with others. Through Bible study, he encountered Jesus personally, and thus Jesus became his God of worship. When Paula Kim asked him during a Bible study if he was certain he would surely enter the Kingdom of Heaven after death, he replied that God would decide solely based on his(Michael's) works.

But Paula explained to him, based on the word of John 5:24, that if he believed in Jesus Christ, he already had eternal life. After this declaration, he never doubted his assurance of salvation. From then on, his faith grew drastically. He longed so much for God's Word that he came to the prayer meeting early in the morning. During his internship in Munich, he continued the Bible study by letter. He worked with us for about three years.

- Peter Ruhnau

He studied law. He studied God's Word with Joseph Kim and regularly attended Sunday worship from 1990 to 1991. Furthermore, he participated in Summer Conference 1990 and Christmas Conference 1990. He successfully completed his studies in 1990. His kindness brought us much joy.

- Wei Mao

She came from China. Samuel Kim had a big heart for Chinese and taught her God's Word. After Samuel Kim flew to China, she studied God's Word with Sara Chang.

- Helga Deutschmann

She was an economics student. She was invited by Grace Sarah Hong to Bible study.

- Irina Stobbe

From the late 1990s onward, she studied the Bible with Grace Sickelmann for several years. After her marriage, she raised her children well, and her family happily lives in the faith.

⋆ Bible Friends 1992-1999

- Sigrid Stefener

She was an athlete. Since 1992, for about two years, she had been intensively studying God's Word with Rebekka Park. At the beginning of 1993, she chose John 5:8, "Jesus said to him, 'Get up, take up your bed, and go!'" as her guiding verse for 1993.

- Joerg Spielfeld

He began studying the Bible with Joseph Kim around April 1993. His prayer topics for 1994 were "Become a good fisher of men, become a disciple of Jesus, and hold firmly to God's Word."

He had already been studying God's Word with Joseph Kim for about a year.

In 1994, our coworkers invited more students to the Bible study. These included Frank(his Bible friend of Andreas S.), Hermann(of Andreas S.), Jochen(Med., of Renate), Ruben, Antje, Inken, Barbara, Jörg, and Sonja.

Bible Friends 1996:

Irina(her Bible friend was Grace Sickelmann), Ingo(Samuel Park), Danny(Samuel Park), Suse(Anja), Christia, Quin, Annemarie(Anja), etc.

⋆ Bible Friends 2000-2005

In 2000, Christoph Bussmann, Emil, Giogia, and some other students studied God's Word.

- Christoph Bussmann

In 2000, Daniel Hong invited him to a personal Bible study. After Daniel Hong moved to Munich, Christoph participated in the group Bible study. Andreas Schmeinck was his friend, and the two maintained a close fellowship until his work took him to

Münster. There, he married a Christian woman.

- Emil

He studied the Bible with Moffat Kim and also with Elisabeth Kim.

- Georgios

He had Bible study with Moffat Kim.

- Giorgia

Since 2000, Giorgia has been the caretaker for the children of David and Mariela from the Schmeinck family. She began studying the Bible regularly with Renate in 2000 and later continued for many years with Esther Choe.

- Christa Unruh

She has studied the Bible with Grace Sickelmann since 2000.

⋆ Bible Friends 2006-2010

- Sang-Hee Park, Gyu-Young Yeon, and Hyeon Lee

Sang-Hee Park(박상희) joined the church in early 2006 at the invitation of Young-Il Choi. She studied God's Word with Peter Bae. After the German course, Sang-Hee Park studied in Düsseldorf and moved there.

In early 2006, Sang-Hee Park invited Gyu-Young Yeon(연규영) to church. Gyu-Young Yeon then invited his friend Hyeon Lee(

이현). Gyu-Young Yeon and Hyeon Lee studied the Bible with Kaleb Lee. Gyu-Young Yeon received a place to study dentistry in East Germany and moved there. Hyeon Lee returned to Korea.

- Seung-Il Oh(오승일)

Seung-Il Oh was a doctoral student in Protestant theology. From autumn 2007 to 2008, he and I studied the Word of God together weekly, from the Gospel of John and the Book of Genesis. He helped us obtain permission to use the hall of the "Euroeck" student residence free of charge for our Easter and Christmas worships.

- Philip

He studied theology with the goal of becoming a teacher. From autumn 2007, he studied God's Word with Kaleb Lee and occasionally attended Sunday worship.

- Na-Ra Hong(홍나라)

Since the beginning of 2008, she attended Sunday worship and studied God's Word with Johanna Lee for about a year.

- Ji-Woong Park(박지웅)

He came from Korea in the early winter semester of 2008 and, on the recommendation of Joshua Kim from Moldova, attended the Sunday worships and studied the Bible with Kaleb Lee. After about a year, he returned to Korea.

⋆ **Bible Friends 2011-2012**

From November 2011, **Jimmy** attended our Sunday worships and Saturday Bible study groups for about a year. He initiated an invitation campaign to invite people to the church. Through this, God encouraged us to actively invite people to worship and faith. **Annette**, his wife, also attended the Sunday worship for a while.

From April 29, 2012, **Mega** from Indonesia faithfully attended our Sunday worship. He returned to Indonesia in the summer of 2012. **Michael** from Africa attended our Sunday worship for about a year. **Bianca** participated in our Sunday worship and Bible study from October 2012 to November 2013. She was a great encouragement to us all.

Since Sunday, November 18, 2012, **Tim Morris**, an exchange student from England, attended Bible study on Saturdays and Sunday worships. He became a good friend of ours. His parents from England attended our Sunday worship on December 2, 2012.

⋆ **Open Cooking Courses and Alpha Courses 2013-2019**

- Cooking Course and Alpha Course 2013

On Saturday, April 20, 2013, at 5:30 p.m., **the first Cooking Course** was held in our student church in Bochum. **Dunja** brought along some international fellow students.

Following the Cooking Course, we launched the **Alpha Course** for seekers in June 2013, which was blessed by God.

Participants in the Cooking & Alpha Course were(as of approximately June 2013):

Dunja, Kaito Nakamura(from Japan), Denis Shakirova(Bulgaria), Wen-Lin(Taiwan), Omran Alsaivari(Syria), Anwat Khamsri(Indonesia), Enrico Taguebou(Cameroon), Tim Morris, etc.

Many students attended the Alpha Course during the summer semester of 2014.

- Participants in the Alpha Course, SS 2014, were:

Wen-Lin(Thailand), Omran Alsaidawo(Syria), Denis Shakirova(Bulgaria), Anwat Khamsri(Thailand), Kaito Nakamura(Japan), Dunja Sharbat Dar(Germany), Enrico Taguebou(Cameroon), Parandoush-Forouzandch(Iran), Christian Becker(Germany), Basel Fkhaida(Palestine), Bah Amadou Tidiana(Guinea), Winsa Alida(Benin), Ynmar Yousef(Syria), Okyanos Atlas(Türkiye), Yana Ivanova(Bulgaria), Ahmet Tahta(Türkiye), Oynsuvad Undur-Origil(Mongolia), Enkhtaivan Enkhzaya Zaya(Mongolia), Abbasi Leila(Iran), Sonja(moved to Uni Tübingen), Aida(moved to Uni Münster)

- Participants of the Alpha Course, WS 2014/15

In addition to some of the participants mentioned above, such as Denis, the following individuals also participated:

Isaac Adjei Safo(Ghana), Vitalii Natsik(Moldova), Yan Chen(China), Elli(Iran), Joel Acipass(Germany), Markus(Germany), Cedric C Paude(Congo), Akbar Yousef(Iran), Johanna Florenz(Colombia), Jsmail, Parminder Singh(India), Oogii(Mongolia), Leila Abbasi(Iran), etc.

- Participants of the Alpha Course, SS 2015

Denis, Vitalii, Joel(Denis and Joel also presented about Bulgaria in the Alpha course), Cedric Hounsanou, Suufy, Yurim Sim, Akbar Yousef(Iran), Markus, Jsmail, Yan, Faith(South Africa; she returned to Paris on September 6), Oogii, Zaya, Enrico, Oyuka(August 18), Faith, Johanna, Yan(attended the Bible study on Saturdays).

Dunja had returned from her year of study in Japan and began attending Sunday Worship regularly in October 2015.

One-to-one Bible Study Group: **Yan** with Esther(during summer), **Yurim** with Renate, and **Zaya** with Renate(starting August 27).

On September 6, Yurim led nine Koreans to Sunday worship: Chan-Il Chung(정찬일) & Eun-Hee Lim(임은희) with their three daughters, Eu-Young Chung(정의영), Seong-Young Chung(정성영), and Hye-Young Chung(정혜영). Yurim also invited Joan Koo(구조은) & Karl and several other Koreans.

Bora Kim(김보라) & Mark Morocz were married on September 19, 2015, in Hungary. Kaleb Lee and I were present.

- Participants of the Alpha Course and the Sunday Worship 2016:

Eslami Pirharati Mahmoud(Iran), Deborah Deer(Hungary), Marvin Dieckmann(Germany), Joan Gyo-Eun Koo(구교은) & Karl, Chan-Il Chung's Family(5 persons), Heon-Woo Lee(이헌우), Hee-Ji Yang(양희지), Min-Young Kang(강민영), Dong -Hyeon Kim(김동현), Kai Rohs, Valeria Cano(Colombia), Rawad Bassil(Syria, Christian), Chan-Song Lee(이찬송),

Vatalii Natsik(Moldova)

- Participants of the Alpha Course and the Sunday Worship 2017. (Some names are missing from this list.)

Dong-A Jang(장동아), Seung-Won Kim(김승원), Hyeon-A Kim(김현아, from Stuttgart) & her fiancé from Dortmund, and Ae-Rin Cho(조애린).

- Participants of the Alpha Course and the Sunday Worship 2018

Sanin, Jeji(예지, friend of Chansong Lee), Lisanne Alissha, Maede and Tahere(daughter and mother from Iran), Lydia(invited by David), Sin-Young(신영), Irina & their three children(Easter Sunday worship), Sirin, You-Mi Cho(조유미), Ji-Eun(지은), Subinth, Franki, Pouneh, Jay, Valeria Cano(Colombia), Valeria's brother

- Participants of the Alpha Course and the Sunday Worship 2019:

Valeria Cano(Colombia), Darya Afshar(Iran), Saja(Iran), Sarai(Colombia, Valeria's girlfriend), Yule, Aysegül Özen(Iran), 조예빈(Ye-Bin Cho), 박성광(Sung-Kwang Park), 안경호(Kyeong-Ho An), 허동욱(Dong-Ok Heo), Tiancheng Liu, Zohre Nemati, 김다영(Da-Young Kim, wife of Heon Woo Lee), 현경(Hyun-Kyung), 권선경(Seon-Kyeong Kwon), 김도훈(Do-Houn Kim)

4. Presentation of the CMI Church in the Evangelical Theology Faculty of the Ruhr University Bochum

On Thursday, June 28, 2012, I presented our church's work

at the seminar of the Evangelical Theological Department of the Ruhr University Bochum. The seminar, entitled "Korean Protestant Churches in Germany - A Positioning," took place on June 28 and 29, 2012. It was organized by Dr. Esther Hornung, who occasionally attended our Sunday worship. She had invited me to give a presentation. There were presentations from three Korean churches and our CMI Church in Bochum. I spoke about the origins of CMI Germany and the history of CMI Dortmund and Bochum for about 30 minutes. After that, I answered questions from the participants.

5. List of Korean Missionaries and a Chinese Missionary in Bochum

The following missionaries have served the Lord in Bochum since 1987:

Our family moved from Dortmund to Bochum on February 28, 1987.

Joseph & Paula Kim moved from Dortmund to Bochum in mid-1987.

In June 1999, this family moved to Duisburg when Joseph Kim accepted a position as a research assistant at the University of Duisburg.

Thomas Hwang(황 토마스) and **Sarah Oh(오 사라)** arrived from Korea on March 24, 1988.

Abraham Oh(오 아브라함) and **Maria Hwang**(황 마리아) arrived in Germany on March 29, 1989, with Maria Junior and Joo-Hand, the babies of Maria and Thomas.

The Hwang family moved to Münster in November 1994 for the student evangelization there.

Later, they moved to Bremen after Thomas Hwang found employment with Kia Motors. When Kia Motors relocated its headquarters to Frankfurt a.M., the family moved via Gießen to Mühltal, a suburb of Darmstadt, in July 1999.

Abraham and Sarah Oh's family also moved to a suburb of Darmstadt after Abraham Oh accepted a job in Frankfurt.

Pauline Lee(김 폴린) arrived from Korea on October 13, 1988. In 1991, she moved to Cologne.

Andreas Lee(이 안드레아스) and **Esther Bae**(배 에스더) arrived on March 29, 1989. **Peter Bae**(배 베드로) arrived on March 19, 1991.

In 2006, the Bae family, Peter and Esther, moved to a Korean church in Bochum. Later, they attended the Free Evangelical Church in Bochum-Langendreer.

Esther Song(송 에스더) and **Rebekka Park**(박 리브가) arrived on August 23, 1989.

After two and a half years, Esther Song returned to Korea in 1991, married Moses Park, and remained there.

Rebekah Park married **Samuel Park**(박 사무엘) in 1991. Samuel Park arrived in Bochum on May 30, 1992.

Rebekah Park finally returned to Korea in January 2000, and

Samuel Park on March 3, 2000.

Grace Sarah Hong(홍 그레이스 사라) arrived in Bochum on September 6, 1989. **Daniel Hong**(홍 다니엘) arrived on September 23, 1993.

After graduating with a degree in electrical engineering from the University of Bochum, Daniel found employment in Munich. Therefore, his family moved to Munich on June 3, 2001.

Samuel Kim and Hannah Kim(김 사무엘 & 한나) arrived on October 4, 1989, with their two sons, David and Lukas.

Later, the family moved to China.

Hannah Lee(이 한나), the wife of **Andreas Lee**, arrived on April 19, 1990, with her daughter.

Later, the family moved to Hanover after Andreas Lee accepted a job there.

Philia Cho(조 필리아) arrived in 1992.

After two years, she moved to Cologne and married a missionary from Jungang UBF in Korea. The couple flew back to Korea.

Elisabeth Kim(김 엘리사벳) arrived in October 1991. Her husband, **Moffat Kim**(김 모팻), arrived on August 4, 1994.

After Moffat Kim completed his doctoral thesis, the couple returned to Korea with their son Lukas on February 23, 2003, when Moffat found employment with LG.

Lydia Lee(이 리디아) moved from Essen to Bochum in 1994. She then moved to Cologne.

Ludger Sickelmann moved from Krefeld to Bochum in June 1990. After completing his computer course as a computer specialist, he married **Grace Sickelmann** at the end of 1990. Grace arrived from Korea on April 2.

This couple moved to Essen on November 9, 2002, and helped many students with the Bible study there. Ludger works as a teacher at a school, and Grace also works as a teacher.

This couple prays for the establishment of a Christian school.

Grace raised her three daughters well and, thanks to Ludger's encouragement, she overcame language and cultural barriers to find a job at the school, where she teaches children with learning difficulties. She also attended a theological seminary and became a pastor.

On October 17, 2021, a house church opened, and she preached at the worship. It's a miracle of the Holy Spirit.

Paul Chang and Sara Chang(장 바울 & 사라) moved from Dortmund to Bochum on February 16, 1995.

When Paul Chang got a job in Frankfurt, this family moved to Darmstadt on July 16, 1999.

Abraham Park and Sarah Park(박 아브라함 & 사라) began attending Sunday worship in Bochum on January 23, 2000. This family moved from Aachen to Bochum in February 2002.

When Abraham Park got a job in Frankfurt, this family moved

to Frankfurt on August 24, 2004.

Young-Il Choi(최영일) and **Yoon-Hee Koo**(구윤희) arrived on May 26, 2000. Yoon-Hee Koo joined the Sickelmann's family as a babysitter and stayed in Essen for a year before returning.

Young-Il Choi received his doctorate in Dortmund and returned.

Kaleb Lee(이 갈렙) arrived in late August 2000, and his pregnant wife, **Johanna Lee**(이 요한나), arrived on October 18, 2000.

In 2021, this family moved to a suburb of Düsseldorf, near Johanna's workplace.

Jakob Zheng came from China in 2000, received his doctorate from the University of Essen, and has been working at BASF in Wiesbaden since 2011.

A total of **33 missionaries** served the Lord here in Bochum, including **14 married couples** and **5 single missionaries**.

Thirteenth Story: Ten Reasons for My Gratitude!

"And Mary said, 'My soul glorifies the LORD, and my spirit rejoices in God my Savior; for he has seen the lowliness of his maid. Behold, from now on all children's children will call me blessed.'" (Luke 1:46-48)

October 3, 2010, was Thanksgiving Day in Germany. During the Sunday worship that day, I shared my "10 Reasons for My Gratitude to God." These reasons are still valid today. That is why I am presenting them here.

1. Thank God for His creation. He created a beautiful world and me, gave me a loving family, good friends, grateful teachers, and faithful helpers, and led me to His grace.

2. Thank God for Jesus Christ, His salvation, and the living hope. He planted the seeds of faith in me through my third and fourth sisters. Then, through friends in my hometown like Yeon-Soo Park(박연수), Jae-Bum Lee(이재범), and Eun-Chun Lee(이은춘), He prepared my heart for faith. Finally, He led me to faith through our church in Daejeon.

3. Thank God for the selfless love of my parents and siblings. My mother, my father, my older brother, and my four sisters lovingly cared for me. When I was one and a half years old, my father passed away after helping with the funeral of a neighbor who had died of an infectious disease.

4. Thank God for So-Hee Yeon(연소희), my sixth-grade teacher. He enabled me to attend middle school despite the poverty. Without his help, I would have become a lumberjack. I also thank God for Jin-Hae Son, my middle school teacher, for his encouragement, and for Seung-Tak Baek(백승탁), the principal of Yesan High School, for his support and scholarship. I thank God for Prof. Bo-Sung Rhee(이보성), who supported me during my master's studies. I thank God for Prof. Schecker of the University of Dortmund for his kind supervision of my dissertation.

5. Thank God for Eun-Chun Lee(이은춘) and his parents, who provided me a free room in Daejeon, my university city. I also thank God for the encouragement of Ho Kang(강호), my friend from my university days.

6. Thank God for Soo-Min Lee(이수민), who invited me to our church in Daejeon. I thank God that Kyoung-Sook Cho(조경숙) taught me how to pray to God on the first day of my church visit. God helped me to believe in Jesus through Peter Suh and supported me through Bona Hong, Namsik Woo(우남식), John Park(박요한), Abraham Kim(김 아브라함), and Isaac Kim(김 이삭), among others. I also thank God for the help of In-Seop Lim(임인섭). Thank God for the warm cooperation of Joo-Yeon Kim(

김주연), Myeong-Hee Han(한명희), Seok-Hee Choi(최석희), Ruth Ahn(안 룻), Hyeo-Soon Kim(김혜순), Myeong-Sook Yang(양명숙), Soon-Ok You(유순옥), Dong-Ju Lee(이동주), Seong-Soo Han(한성수), Myeong-Ja Kim(김명자), Hak-Young & Helen Ryu(오학영 & 류헬렌), Ki-Wook Koo(구기욱), Joon-Chan Cho(조준찬), Soo-Cheol Lee(이수철), Soo-Young Lee(이수영), Sook-Hee Jeong(정숙희), etc.

7. Thank God for the blessing of family with Esther in 1977. Esther is a devoted and good woman. Thanks to God's blessing of two sons, Stephan and Timothée. God blessed Stephan and Marie Seungmi so that they could start a family in March 2009. With God's help, Stephan got a good job, and Marie Seungmi finished her studies in college. They raise their two children, Sophia and Sean, well. Timothée graduated from the university, works in a good firm, and has married lovely Monica.

8. God assigned us to the student mission in Dortmund and Bochum through the cooperation of Korean and German co-workers: e.g. Martin Nachtrodt, Ludger, Martin R., Walter, K-H, Di & El, H-P(Dortmund); Hartmut, Anja, Ulrike, Stephanie, Stephan Schulzki etc.(Bochum); Doo-Kyoo Kim & Dong-Ok(Rheda & Dortmund), Hie-Za Kim(김희자, Rheda), Youkang Hur(허유강), Paul&Sara Chang(Do & Bo), Lydia Lee(Essen & Dortmund), Andreas & Ruth Ahn(Do), Joseph&Paula Kim(Do & Bo), Isaiah&Bekkie Lee, Joseph & Rebecca Han, Ki-Min Lee(DO); Thomas & Maria Hwang, Abraham & Sarah Oh, Peter & Esther Bae, Pauline Lee, Daniel & Grace Hong, Esther Song, Samuel & Rebekka Park, Samuel & Hannah Kim, Andreas

& Hannah Rhee, Moffat & Elisabeth Kim, Yoon-Hee Gu, Abraham-Elia & Sarah Park, Jacob Cheng, Young-Il Choi, Kaleb & Johanna Lee.(BO), etc. have contributed. God has encouraged us through Isaac Lee, Paulus Kwon, Joshua Lee, Joseph Lee, etc.

9. God has called Andreas, Renate, Caleb, Johanna, David, Mariela, Johanna, Josephine, and others, and uses them as precious co-workers in the ministry of the Gospel.

10. God has given us the vision to use ourselves and our church to be a blessing to Bochum, Europe, and the whole world. He will multiply us greatly and, through us, bless Germany and the entire world.

Fourteenth Story: Esther's Victory in Returning Home and Fellowship with Me

"He is not the God of the dead, but of the living, for to Him all are alive."
(Luke 20:38)

Although physically frail, Esther was generally healthy. However, around September 2018, while standing on the car roadway of Semperstraße near the bus stop "Am Eurenkampstraße," she saw a student riding his bicycle quickly down Semperstraße from Markstraße. She tried to avoid the bicycle, but she fell backward and hit her back against the curb between the car roadway and the sidewalk. She had pain in her back and also in her stomach. For this reason, with the help of Dr. Renate Schmeinck, she got a doctor's appointment at a practice in Hattingen. On the day of our wedding anniversary in 2018, we drove to the doctor for her examination.

On October 18, we went to the doctor again to find out the results of the examination. She entered to the doctor's office, and I waited in the car. When she returned, she initially said nothing.

When we came to our church and I was just about to get out of the car, she said she had stomach cancer. She hadn't told me this until then to avoid my panic and prevent a car accident.

Esther underwent stomach cancer surgery on October 29, 2018, at the Augusta Hospital in Bochum and then received four chemotherapy treatments at the doctor's office in front of Bochum's Main Train Station.

When her hair started falling out, she shaved her head and put a scarf on it. Esther humorously testified to the Gospel to doctors, nurses, and visitors, "With my bald head I look like a Buddhist monk, and with a scarf on my head I look like a Muslim woman. But my heart is Christian."

After chemotherapy, Esther underwent three weeks of rehab in Bad Oeningen. After returning from rehab, she stayed at home. However, she lost a lot of weight because she could not eat properly. So, she started getting the nutrients she needed through a tube. She had to go to the hospital several times. Her condition continued to deteriorate over time while she stayed at home. She slept in the living room, and I slept in the bedroom. She often moaned in pain in the middle of the night, like Job in the Old Testament. But Esther didn't want me to get out of bed and help her because she didn't want to wake me from my sleep.

When I attended the Summer Bible Conference for three days in early August, our youngest son, Timothée, took extra leave to stay with Esther. He slept in the bedroom, and Esther slept in the living room. At midnight, she felt severe pain, but she didn't wake Timothée. So, she pretended not to be in pain.

She forbade me from telling her relatives, especially her older sister, about her illness. She wanted to prevent her older sister from falling into great grief. So, I didn't tell her relatives until a few days before she went home to Heavenly Father. Esther said that our eldest son, Stephan, and his family should not come from the USA so that they would not be burdened by her illness. Esther also didn't want missionaries who lived far away from Bochum or in Korea to visit her so that they wouldn't be burdened. Despite this, Bo-Young Lim(임보영) came from my mother church in Daejeon, Korea; Esther was naturally grateful to her for the visit.

On Wednesday, November 20, 2019, at around 6 a.m., Esther was in unbearable pain and had to be taken to the Knappschaft hospital in Bochum-Langendreer by ambulance at around 7:30 a.m. At that point, Esther had already prepared her heart to go to Heavenly Father. She didn't tell me that, of course, but I could hear her answer when a doctor asked her about the purpose of the treatment.

In the hospital, Esther's condition gradually deteriorated.

On the morning of Monday, December 9, 1919, the doctor offered to inject Esther with morphine. But I replied that I would first listen to the opinion of our two sons when they came in the evening and give him an answer. So, Esther did not receive the morphine solution on the 9th, but only on the morning of

December 10th.

From Monday(December 9) to Tuesday(December 10) at midnight, Esther fought a fierce spiritual and physical battle and won the battle.

I was also with her in her hospital bedroom at night. With great pain, Esther asked God several times, "Why do I have to suffer this?" Afterwards, she called three times, "Dad, Dad, Dad!" "Dad" was Esther's way of referring to "God." After that, she said three times, "Forgive me!" I think that she asked God for forgiveness because she complained about her illness. Having said this, Esther had a miraculous, peaceful face and soon fell asleep. Those were the last words I heard from Esther. From then on, Esther slept peacefully until she went to God at 4 p.m. on December 13, 2019.

Esther encouraged many people to believe in Jesus Christ by testifying to them about Him at every opportunity, even during her illness. On the day of her passing, a miracle happened. Esther had prayed for a long time for Mrs. Marian, who lives on the third floor of our apartment, and had repeatedly explained the Gospel to her whenever she had the opportunity. However, the woman had replied that she could not believe in Jesus because of her rational thinking. On December 13, around noon, four hours before Esther was to go home, Mrs. Marian came into the sickroom and confessed that she now believed in Jesus and in the resurrection of the dead and that this was only possible with help from above.

Esther's resting place. I will be here with her later.

On the tombstone, it says,
"Jesus said to her, 'I am the resurrection and the life. The one who believes in me will live, even though they die.'"
John 11:25
The Choe Couple

God didn't want me to feel lonely after Esther fell asleep, so He gave me the conviction that the resurrected Esther will always accompany me like an angel, and her presence in my heart does encourage me. That's why I live with joy, knowing that Esther is always with me and accompanies me. This must, of course, be understood in terms of the heavenly concept of time, which is different from the earthly concept of time and results from a life of faith in the resurrection. I believe that the resurrected Esther is more beautiful than any of the most stunning images from her previous life. I live in faith in the resurrection and enjoy walking with the risen Esther, looking at her gracious image again and again, and praising God. And I pray that the Good News of Christ's resurrection will be preached to the end of the world.

"Jesus said to her, 'I am the resurrection and the life. The one who believes in me will live, even though they die; and whoever lives by believing in me will never die. Do you believe this?'"

(John 11:25-26)

"But you will receive power when the Holy Spirit comes on you; and you will be my witnesses in Jerusalem, and in all Judea and Samaria, and to the ends of the earth."

(Acts 1:8)